CHALLENGES

The life &
teachings of
VENERABLE
MASTER
CHENG YEN

CHALLENGES

GARY HO

Douglas & McIntyre
D&M PUBLISHERS INC.
Vancouver/Toronto

09 10 11 12 13 5 4 3 2 1

Douglas & McIntyre
A division of D&M Publishers Inc.
2323 Quebec Street, Suite 201
Vancouver BC Canada V5T 4S7
www.dmpibooks.com

Library and Archives Canada Cataloguing in Publication
Ho, Gary, 1947–
Challenges: The Life and Teachings of Venerable Master Cheng Yen / Gary Ho.

ISBN 978-1-55365-216-8

1. Zhengyan, Shi. 2. Fo jiao ci ji ci shan shi ye ji jin hui. 3. International relief.
4. Buddhism—Taiwan—Charities. 5. Buddhist nuns—Taiwan—Biography.
6. Women philanthropists—Taiwan—Biography. 7. Taiwan—Biography. i. Title.

BQ946.E547H62 2009   294.3092 C2008-906383-X

Editing by Douglas Shaw and Lucy Kenward
Cover and text design by Naomi MacDougall
Cover photograph by Juan I-Jong, courtesy of the Tzu Chi Foundation

Printed and bound in Canada by Friesens
Printed on acid-free paper that is forest friendly (100% post-consumer
recycled paper) and has been processed chlorine free

We gratefully acknowledge the financial support of the Canada Council for the Arts,
the British Columbia Arts Council, the Province of British Columbia through the
Book Publishing Tax Credit, and the Government of Canada through the Book Publishing
Industry Development Program (BPIDP) for our publishing activities.

CONTENTS

{ Preface

A FRIEND ONCE REMARKED that whenever I talk about Tzu Chi, known in English as the Buddhist Compassion Relief Tzu Chi Foundation, my eyes shine with joy. Long before I joined the organization, since my school days in fact, I have harbored an aspiration to live out the altruistic spirit of the great sages: to help the poor and to bring peace of mind to people. After years of searching, I finally came across the Tzu Chi Foundation and its Taiwanese founder, Master Cheng Yen. The better I understand Tzu Chi's beliefs, the more frequently I participate in its charitable missions. I know that I have found a way to realize my aspiration.

Twenty-one years have passed since I joined Tzu Chi. At first I kept my involvement at a distance so that I could scrutinize the foundation and Master Cheng Yen objectively and rationally. By adopting this stance, I reasoned, I could reflect on my actions and remind myself to be mindful of my own conduct. Through this process, I came to identify with Tzu Chi even more.

Throughout the years, I have often placed myself in the Master's shoes and pondered what I would have done if faced with the same challenges. Any number of times I thought I had better methods and solutions than the Master. Yet time and again, I have been proven wrong. I have come to realize how wise the Master's decisions are.

I have seen how resolute the Master is when facing setbacks or misunderstandings, and how persistent she is when facing unbearable pressure. She may be petite and frail, but she is unbelievably determined. She may look gentle and speak softly, but she works vigorously. Looking at the Master, I finally understand the meaning of the Chinese saying, "Those who can endure unspeakable hardship are truly forged of iron."

Master Cheng Yen is a wise, compassionate Buddhist nun who practices what she teaches. She often treats traditional Chinese culture with affection and respect, and at the same time she revitalizes it through contemporary language and interpretation. The Master has made enormous contributions to humankind by giving unselfishly, by using to advantage the current affluent social conditions in Taiwan, and by harnessing the support of countless people both in Taiwan and abroad. The Master's influence transcends time and space.

Her philosophy is that when suffering people are touched by the unprejudiced, genuine concern shown by fellow human beings, they will open up their own hearts and find love within. Thus, they may eventually move from being helped to helping others, thereby bringing the cycle of goodness full circle.

The altruistic spirit of Master Cheng Yen and her humanitarian care for all human beings are well worthy of our respect. It's truly my honor to recommend her to all readers of this book and to follow in her footsteps on the Path of the Bodhisattvas. I believe that if people in every part of the globe practiced the ideals of Master Cheng Yen and the Tzu Chi Foundation in earnest, our world would be free of violence, ill will, and hatred. Instead, it would become a place of compassion, selfless giving, and love. (Tzu Chi members never preach Buddhism while they do relief works, though. To the Tzu Chi people, embracing the Buddha is a very personal thing. You're welcome to do so, of course, but you're not urged to.)

The Master has successfully applied Buddhist wisdom to modern life through active participation in serving the world. The Master inspired me, as she has many, many others. Through serving, I can see the Buddha reincarnate in the bodies of Tzu Chi volunteers. Fulfilling one's earthly duty to serve other human beings is how we realize the essence of Buddhism. To Tzu Chi, compassion is all about action.

I believe wisdom is universal. And I believe the spirit of altruism and gratification should be shared with Canadians. I'd like to relay the Master's messages of loving our world and our environment to our Canadian friends, thereby helping us achieve spiritual peacefulness. That was the motivation for me to write this book.

I am indebted to my friend Kao Hsin-chiang, who has contributed much to the media and culture of Taiwan and—through his knowledge, writing ability, and editing skills—to the publication of this book.

Shortly after I introduced Kao to Tzu Chi in early 1989, he resigned as president of *China Times Express* to become a volunteer at Tzu Chi. Since then, he has organized and written articles about Tzu Chi, written the lyrics for the anthem of the Tzu Chi Junior College of Nursing (now the Tzu Chi College of Technology), and designed a poster for recruiting students. Moreover, he generated the original media interest in the organization by inviting Taiwanese celebrities and his friends in the press to visit the city of Hualien in eastern Taiwan to learn about the history and current missions of Tzu Chi. The major local newspapers and magazines printed stories about Tzu Chi, and the local people began to pay attention as well, and this led to the publication of *Still Thoughts*, a book of Master Cheng Yen's famous quotations compiled by Kao and me. The book was well received by Taiwan's readers: in just a few years it was reprinted three hundred times and 60,500 copies were sold, a record in Taiwan that hasn't been surpassed.

I am also thankful to Shi Fang-yu, who helped draw up the first draft of this book. To ensure its accuracy, she read numerous related books, verified hundreds of facts, and assisted me in the compilation. She showed me the professionalism of a news reporter, and her patience and diligence made a formidable impression on me.

All Tzu Chi volunteers are my teachers and my role models. This book expresses my respect to them.

Finally, I would like to thank my wife, Kuo Shu-yuan, who introduced Tzu Chi to me. She continually supports and encourages me to walk joyously on the path of Tzu Chi. When I am tired from work, she comforts me; when I am busy, she helps me. She shares my burdens, grief, hopes, and joy. She is truly my best companion and guide on the path of Tzu Chi.

This Is Master Cheng Yen

Master Cheng Yen has engaged in spiritual cultivation for over forty years. She calls herself a "mere nun," but she works in and for this world with an otherworldly spirit.

Founded by the Master in 1966, the Tzu Chi Foundation has grown into an international charitable and relief organization that has ten million members worldwide with an army of one million volunteers. The so-called Tzu Chi "commissioners"—a word derived from the phrase "committed volunteers"—dedicate their time and money to bringing peace and joy to those who suffer, regardless of their race, religious background, or citizenship.

Simply put, the Chinese words "Tzu Chi" mean "compassion and relief"—in other words, compassion in action. The work of Master Cheng Yen and Tzu Chi revive the centuries-old, original mission of Buddhism under the banner of "Humanistic Buddhism." To the Master, indulging only in self-cultivation does not make one a true Buddhist. A Buddhist should be compassionate about the world and its people, identify with others' suffering, and be committed to take actions that ease their pain.

MASTER CHENG YEN was born Wang Chin-yun on May 14, 1937, in Chingshui, a small town in central Taiwan. Her father was a cinema owner, and the family led a wealthy, comfortable existence.

However, a major event changed Wang Chin-yun's life at age twenty-three. Her father had high blood pressure. One day, he complained to his daughter about a severe headache. She called for the doctor, who gave her father a shot, which brought his blood pressure down somewhat. When the doctor left, Wang Chin-yun took her father home in their family pedicab. When they reached their destination, though, her father had lost the ability to walk. He couldn't even talk. The next day, her father died of a brain hemorrhage.

The death of her father shattered her world. Not only was she stricken with grief, she also blamed herself for her father's death. For days, she walked around like a zombie, repeatedly asking, "Where is my father now?"

She went to a nearby temple every day and began to consider becoming a Buddhist nun. This was not an easy decision, though, since she was the oldest child in the family, her mother was in poor health, and her younger brothers and sisters needed to be taken care of.

At the temple, Wang Chin-yun met a nun, Master Hsiu Tao, who became her mentor. The two wandered to wherever their spirits led them. They stayed at several temples on the east coast of Taiwan. Back then, in 1961, the area was desolate and undeveloped, and the residents were poor. Eventually, the two travelers discovered a tiny, run-down temple in a forest neighboring a poor village. They settled here and led an ascetic life.

In a rather revolutionary break from the Buddhist tradition, Wang Chin-yun and Master Hsiu Tao decided not to accept any alms or offerings from the local people, who they believed were suffering too much to be able to make donations. Instead, the pair raised their own vegetables, collected wild plants and fruits, and foraged for leftover peanuts and sweet potatoes from the farmers' fields. Wang Chin-yun felt a sweet joy in this simple life.

In the winter of 1962, a determined Wang Chin-yun made a bold move on her spiritual quest. She shaved her own head, which was a completely untraditional and unorthodox act. She also remained without a master. A nun without a proper master was considered a renegade and was something outside of the protocol.

One Buddhist master eventually took her as his follower in 1963—the Venerable Master Yin Shun. He was an influential thinker. If Master Cheng Yen could be seen as the person who has helped Humanistic Buddhism flourish worldwide, then Master Yin Shun was the mastermind behind the concept.

A motto taught by Master Yin Shun to Master Cheng Yen describes well the fundamental thinking of Humanistic Buddhism: *Devotion to Buddhism, devotion to all beings.*

MASTER CHENG YEN launched the Tzu Chi Foundation within a few years of becoming a follower of Master Yin Shun, and over the following decades, the charitable organization developed and grew into the influential body it is today.

Now more than seventy years old, Master Cheng Yen still works hard every day. The Master is often asked, "How much do you have to do to make this world a peaceful one?" The Master always replies, "If I can't finish the work in this life, I'll return in the next life, and the next life, and the next life, until the work is done."

The Master says to Tzu Chi members on their deathbeds that they shouldn't be saddened by death, for they will come back in the next life and serve again. She says to them, "Go now. Come back soon."

This is real Buddhism in action. To Master Cheng Yen and her followers, the ultimate goal isn't going to heaven and living there happily ever after. Their commitment to altruism and self-lessness has led to a belief that they will reincarnate to serve again, life after life.

one

A TOUGH BEGINNING

1 } *Making the Great Resolution*

CHALLENGE: Is it possible to uphold one's
principles when one barely has enough to eat?

"Adversity is like the grindstone used for polishing
jade: if you don't use it, the jade won't shine."
MASTER CHENG YEN

Background

Today Tzu Chi is a popular, well-supported organization. Master
Cheng Yen's followers are all over the world, but few people know
that forty years ago, she had nothing. Leading an ascetic life, the
petite nun wholeheartedly carried out her spiritual cultivation in
a tiny wooden hut behind Pu Ming Temple in Hualien, located
on the east coast of Taiwan. Despite her destitution, she resolved
not to accept disciples, not to accept offerings from followers, and
not to perform Buddhist rituals to earn money.

Although it was always a matter of course for Buddhist monks
and nuns to ask for alms and receive offerings from lay followers, Master Cheng Yen decided to uphold the conviction of Zen
Master Pai Chang (720–814): "No work, no meal." Even though
she was penniless and had no skills to make a living, she resolutely
chose to decline all offerings—a choice that brought her much
hardship and suffering.

Challenge

Is it possible to hold firm to one's principles when they are at odds with the harsh reality that one has no money or food? "No" is the answer for most people, but "yes" was the Master's reply. Instead of recoiling from the hardship and withdrawing from her principles, she searched unrelentingly for different ways to support herself.

First, she grew vegetables, a skill she had acquired while staying at Tzu Yun Yen Temple before she became a nun. In 1965, the Master and three other disciples had plowed the barren fields behind Pu Ming Temple to grow peanuts and vegetables to feed themselves. They spent the whole day working in the field with the only exception of studying sutras. Master Cheng Yen's first disciple, Te Tzu, was extraordinarily unyielding in the face of difficulties. When Te Tzu was unable to borrow a water buffalo from nearby farmers, she simply took its place, put the heavy yoke on her shoulders, and started plowing the field.

Even with such hard work, food was scarce and living quarters were cramped. Often the revenue earned from the crops—they sold what was left after consumption—was not enough to pay for the fertilizer needed to grow them. Sometimes, Master Cheng Yen and the other three nuns had only some white rice and a small piece of tofu cut into four pieces and soaked in salty water for dinner. The single bed they shared was so tiny that to fit on it the four of them had to lie on their sides and huddle together like shrimps.

Since farming alone could not earn them enough money for food, the Master sold sweaters she had knitted, concrete sacks she had converted into small animal feed bags, chrysanthemums she had grown, and baby shoes, cotton gloves, clothes, diapers, ceramics, and plastic flowers that she had made. She and the other nuns tried every possible means to earn a little income.

Even today, the nuns at the Abode of Still Thoughts, the headquarters of the Tzu Chi Foundation, still uphold the rule of "No work, no meal." They grow vegetables, make candles, and produce bean powder, a sort of dietary supplement. Royalties from Master Cheng Yen's books are also an important source of revenue for the nuns.

Effects and Reflections

For the past forty years, the self-sufficiency of the Master and her followers has had a great influence on all Tzu Chi members. Seeing that the Master and the other nuns declined all offerings, gritted their teeth, and sustained themselves through the most destitute times, Tzu Chi members are certain that the nuns would never put a penny of donations into their own pockets. Such selfless devotion has won the respect of all members and as a result has inspired them to donate wholeheartedly their money and time for charitable activities.

The journey of life is not always a smooth ride. Many people have been defeated by or have compromised with the setbacks they faced. However, Master Cheng Yen chose resolutely to walk on the path that she felt was right. She set a good example for us to follow—we should not quit easily when our choices and principles are bitterly challenged by hardships and difficulties. Many great thinkers, scientists, religious practitioners, or social reformers throughout history fearlessly and joyfully upheld their resolutions regardless of the adversity and trials life brought to them. Eventually, they broke through the valley of darkness and shed light onto the world. Because of them, civilization has developed and human glory has shone forth.

2 } *The Tzu Chi Foundation is born*

CHALLENGE: Can one carry through a
moment of enthusiasm to long-term action?

"Knowledge begins actions, while actions complete knowledge."
WANG YANG-MING, 15TH-CENTURY CHINESE PHILOSOPHER

Background

We tend to sympathize with people in unfortunate circumstances,
but how many of us transform this feeling into concrete actions
and reach out to help the needy? And what kinds of strength can
such sympathy generate?

In 1966, Master Cheng Yen was visiting the sick father of a
follower in a hospital in Fenglin Township. On her way out of the
ward, she saw a pool of blood on the floor and wondered where
it had come from. She inquired and was told that it had been left
behind by a Taiwanese aboriginal woman who had had a miscar-
riage. The woman's relatives had carried her for eight hours from
their remote mountain village to the hospital, only to be turned
away because they could not pay the security deposit of US$200.

The Master's heart ached when she heard this story. For a long
time she worried whether that aboriginal woman was dead or alive.
The incident taught her the importance of money in doing charitable work and prompted her to raise money to save the suffering.

14

Challenge

For a nun who refused to accept offerings from followers or perform Buddhist ceremonies for pay, raising funds to help people was no easy task. Yet the vivid memory of the blood left behind by the aboriginal woman prompted Master Cheng Yen to make a vow: she resolved to put the compassionate spirit of Buddhism into action, so that preventable tragedies like this one could be avoided. As the Master thought of Kuan Yin, the Bodhisattva of Compassion—a bodhisattva with a thousand eyes to see the suffering in the world and a thousand hands to reach out to help the needy—she realized that if five hundred kindhearted people could come together, there would be one thousand eyes and one thousand hands. If each of these people extended a helping hand wherever they saw suffering, they would truly be the omnipresent Kuan Yin Bodhisattva.

After careful calculations, the Master explained her plan to her followers. There were four nuns, including the Master, living in the Abode, and two old lay followers. If each of them sewed one pair of baby shoes each day, together they would earn an extra sixty cents a day, which is US$18 each month or US$200 a year. This money would be enough to help someone like the aboriginal woman who'd miscarried. If each of Master Cheng Yen's thirty lay followers were to set aside two cents from their grocery money each day and save it in bamboo "piggy banks," together they would save US$11.25 each month. This idea of saving just two cents from one's grocery money to save a life gradually spread throughout the markets in Hualien and to other counties in Taiwan. More and more people responded to the Master's creative charity campaign, and on March 24, 1966, the Buddhist Compassion Relief Tzu Chi Foundation was established with the purpose of helping the needy.

As time went by, more and more members of the foundation asked Master Cheng Yen to accept them as her disciples. Originally, wanting only to quietly cultivate her own spirituality and not be involved with worldly affairs, she had vowed not to take in disciples. However, to realize her commitment to helping the needy, she withdrew this vow, accepting disciples on condition that they become members of the foundation and shoulder its social relief work. The number of disciples soared rapidly. Consequently, the charity work of the foundation developed step by step.

Effects and Reflections
As the saying goes, "Practicing what one knows is not easy." Indeed, not many people put their thoughts of compassion into action. When seeing the suffering of others or the unfair treatment they are subjected to, we might feel sad or angry. And then what do we do? Do we put our sympathy into action, or just leave it as a thought? The challenge is to take action and make a difference.

Upholding one's principles is hard, but breaking one's strictly held principles and beliefs is even harder. In order to follow the Buddha's teachings and help the poor, Master Cheng Yen quietly dropped her insistence on only doing her own spiritual cultivation and on not accepting disciples. What amazes people is that she could come up with the brilliant idea of saving two cents a day—a wise, simple, and effective way to put the Buddha's compassion into practice. Ever since then, every penny of the donations raised by foundation members has been used for charity work.

Master Cheng Yen has never regretted her choice to devote her life to relieving suffering, and this noble spirit has motivated many people to pitch in and help others through the foundation. Whenever they see someone in need of assistance, Tzu Chi members immediately reach out, with the thought, "If I don't reach out to help, who will?" The story of the pool of blood teaches us that nothing will change if we do not act on the thoughts of compassion and enthusiasm we have at this very moment.

Another example of someone who has made a difference by putting compassion into action is Albert Schweitzer, a great humanitarian of the twentieth century. Although he was an accomplished theologian, philosopher, and musician before the age of thirty, Schweitzer resolved to enroll in medical school after reading an article on the shortage of missionaries and medical facilities in the Congo. After becoming a doctor, he established a hospital in French Equatorial Africa from which he could serve and cure poor, sick people in Africa. Dr. Schweitzer's courage and decisiveness not only realized his ideal of helping the needy, but also continues to inspire people throughout the world. If every one of us could feel for others and bravely reach out to help, then this defiled world could surely become a Pure Land.

3 } *The death of an aid recipient*

CHALLENGE: Why did a good deed of
saving a life turn into a tragedy?

"In addition to love, it takes wisdom and good
methods to do good deeds." MASTER CHENG YEN

Background

The foundation's first aid recipient was an impoverished eighty-
six-year-old grandmother from mainland China who lived alone
with no one to take care of her. When the case was reported to
the foundation, Tzu Chi members immediately went to provide
her with clothing, food, and medical help so that she could better
enjoy the final years of her life. When she passed away, the foundation organized her funeral. This set a precedent for the future
care of Tzu Chi's aid recipients.

The second aid recipient was Mrs. Huang Tan-kuei, who
was afflicted with glaucoma. When her case was reported to the
foundation, the Huang family was too poor to feed themselves,
let alone afford her eye surgery. Although the nuns could barely
support themselves, the foundation still decided to pay for the
surgery, which would cost US$125. Unexpectedly, the surgery was
not successful; however, Tzu Chi members did not stop offering

the family help. To ease the Huangs' financial strain, the foundation gave them rice and US$30 toward medical fees each month. The monetary aid was gradually reduced as Mr. Huang's income grew, until he earned enough to support the family. Members of the foundation believed that they had helped Mrs. Huang overcome the hardest period in her life.

To everyone's surprise, shortly after the aid was suspended Mrs. Huang committed suicide.

Challenge

Why did this happen? Tzu Chi members were upset and wanted to know the reasons for the tragedy. It seems that Mr. Huang brought home three small cabbages, hoping his wife could use them over three days. Without being aware of her husband's intention, Mrs. Huang prepared a special meal for their five children using all of the cabbages in a pot of gruel. In a rage, Mr. Huang severely rebuked his wife for being so wasteful and useless, and she, unable to overcome the humiliation, took her own life.

This death dealt a hard blow to Master Cheng Yen and the Tzu Chi members. The goals of saving the poor and the sick had not been achieved, and a tragedy had occurred.

This heartrending experience reminded the young Master that in addition to love, it takes wisdom and proper planning to do good deeds. Without these, all efforts could be wasted and Tzu Chi's assistance might even aggravate the problem. After much contemplation, she decided that material aid alone cannot solve problems—what impoverished people truly need is long-term spiritual support. To prevent another tragedy in the future, the Master set a new rule for helping the needy: Tzu Chi members should visit all aid recipients at least once a month. Even after the recipients stop receiving aid from the foundation, they should continue to be given regular care and attention.

Effects and Reflections

To make any system efficient and appropriate, constant evaluation and readjustment are necessary. Although Mrs. Huang's death was not Tzu Chi's fault, it dealt a major blow to its charitable work. Sad but not daunted, the Master was determined to improve the system. She reflected on the event and saw the blind spots in the system.

The Master and her followers learned from this incident that the pursuit of an ideal inevitably involves making mistakes, but the most important thing is to identify and correct these mistakes. In other words, we should "learn while we work and work while we learn." Tzu Chi now emphasizes that both the material and psychological needs of its aid recipients must be attended to. "Commissioners" (referring to the "committed volunteers" handpicked by the Master to carry out the works of Tzu Chi) try their best to visit care recipients at least once a month, if not more frequently, to see if they have enough to eat and wear and, above all, to listen to their complaints, if they have any. Sometimes these volunteers distribute tapes of the Master's lectures or books written by the Master, hoping that those in difficult circumstances can find a way to alleviate their suffering and get back on their feet.

Peter F. Drucker, a master of management and the author of *Managing the Non-Profit Organization: Practices and Principles*, once analyzed three hospitals in a community. He discovered that the least medically sophisticated hospital was, surprisingly, the most highly acclaimed. Care was the key factor in its popularity. From time to time, the hospital would send discharged patients greeting cards, warmly asking after their health and hoping they would never have to come back to the hospital again. Such continuous and thoughtful care touched the heart of the community.

Tzu Chi's follow-up care also conveys to people that the foundation still remembers them. Moreover, face-to-face conversations between Tzu Chi members and those they visit show continuing concern and support for the care recipients, which gives those in need the strength to carry on.

4 } *Working on a larger scale*

CHALLENGE: Can disaster relief be carried out
without a work force, goods, and experience?

"What is faith worth if it is not translated into action?"
MAHATMA GANDHI

Background

On the night of the Mid-Autumn Festival in 1973, Typhoon Nara
unexpectedly struck eastern Taiwan. Fed by the high winds, a
fire spread and engulfed all of Tanan Village in Taitung County.
At the time, Master Cheng Yen was in her hometown in western Taiwan to celebrate her mother's birthday. When she heard
the news on the radio, the Master's heart went out to the villagers, and she left early the following day for Tanan Village. What
she saw there was heartbreaking. The whole village was burned
beyond recognition, most houses were reduced to ashes, and hundreds of people were left homeless. The scale of the tragedy was
far more devastating than the media had reported.

Master Cheng Yen promptly decided to carry out relief work,
and not a second was to be wasted.

Challenge

Lacking experience, human power, and money, how could Tzu
Chi carry out the relief work? The Master immediately called an

emergency meeting. After making a rough evaluation, the participants estimated that a total of us$15,000 would be needed.

To obtain the money, the foundation needed to spread the word. However, two decades ago, the communication networks along Taiwan's east coast were extremely slow. To make matters worse, the media gave this disaster very little coverage, since Taiwan's National Day was just around the corner. Since Taiwan was still under martial law at that time, no one dared offend the authorities by suggesting they focus more attention on the disaster, and consequently people in other regions had no idea how extensive the damage really was. This made mobilizing people and raising funds for the relief work extremely difficult.

At that time, us$15,000 was an astronomical figure to the Tzu Chi members. How could they raise the money in the shortest period of time? Undaunted, Tzu Chi members began to privately distribute fliers, produced by hand by volunteers, to spread the news of the disaster. The method proved useful, as many people indeed donated money. But the amount still fell short. Fortunately, one kindhearted person donated us$7,500 and thus enabled the relief work to proceed.

Immediately the Master bought 148 blankets and hundreds of items of clothing and hired a big truck to deliver the relief supplies to Tanan Village. She believed these would help the victims through their hardships until they could look after themselves. Villagers and local residents were coordinated to distribute the relief goods and emergency funds to 148 affected families. The list of victims' families was determined after site visits by Tsu Chi volunteers. Local authorities also provided Tzu Chi with victim confirmation. The relief work seemed to be a success.

Due to limited funds, Tzu Chi could only help those who needed help the most. When some veterans found out they were not on Tzu Chi's list to receive aid, they became angry. They blocked the bus stop, refusing to let Master Cheng Yen leave. Worried about the Master's safety, her disciples begged her not to meet with the protesters. However, believing that compassion is human nature and that the veterans would understand her decision, she insisted on talking to them.

The Master calmly stepped outside the house where she was staying and spoke with the veterans. Her words *did* calm them down. She said that Tzu Chi members and other Taiwanese people had always respected the veterans' contributions to the nation, and that she believed the Ministry of Defense would help them through this hardship since they had served Taiwan. She explained that because Tzu Chi is a nongovernmental organization, its main function is to complement the government and take care of those the authorities have not attended to. Therefore, Master Cheng Yen explained, Tzu Chi could not help veterans this time because of a shortage of funds, but the Master assured them that she would visit Tanan again. If they had not obtained the help they needed by that time, Tzu Chi would definitely provide them with aid. The Master's explanation quelled the confrontation, and later the Master did indeed fulfill her promises—she returned to Tanan and distributed materials to the veterans.

Effects and Reflections

At a meeting of Tzu Chi's Taiwanese commissioners in 1999, an old man with a well-used blanket in his hands asked to see Master Cheng Yen. Looking at the stranger, the Master was somewhat puzzled. Then the man said, "Master, I'm here to return this blanket." He lifted a corner of the blanket to show the words "Buddhist Tzu Chi Foundation, Hualien" embroidered in red.

The old man had been given the blanket when his home in Tanan Village was destroyed by fire, and it had comforted his family of seven through twenty-six winters. Now things had improved for the family, and they no longer needed the blanket. The grandfather hoped that the warmth this blanket had brought his family could be passed on to the needy year after year, generation after generation, and so he returned the blanket to the Master.

If a lack of experience, people, and money had stopped the Master from carrying out relief work in Tanan Village, it is certain that Tzu Chi would not have had such a long list of successful relief efforts. Her vision and determination paved the way for Tzu Chi. Similarly, when we believe in a worthy cause, we should plan carefully and work with unwavering determination. Most important of all, we should not let inexperience deter us. We will gradually find the way, and wisdom and strength will flow forth.

In the Tang dynasty, the great monk Hsuan-tsang (602–664) vowed to study the profoundness of Buddhism and to enrich the Buddhist scriptures, which were scarce at that time in China. So he set out on an unprecedented journey to India, crossing deserts and foreign lands without a map or guide. What experience or support was there for him to draw upon on a holy mission that had no parallel in history? He met many hardships on the way. But wherever he went, he promulgated the Buddha's teachings and tried to improve people's lives. Because of his steadfast determination, he achieved the unimaginable—translating the Buddhist scriptures into Chinese and writing or compiling a commentary on these texts.

5 } *Lessons from Typhoon Thelma*

CHALLENGE: Must everyone
cooperate when we do good deeds?

"I came to serve, not to be served. " JESUS CHRIST

Background

It took a long time for Taiwan to recover from Typhoon Nara; however, not long after, in 1977, Typhoon Thelma devastated Taiwan even more seriously—a disaster aggravated by human negligence.

One month prior to Thelma, a fierce supertyphoon had swept through the densely populated northern regions of Taiwan. Alerted to its destructive power, residents had taken safety precautions and secured their homes, so the scale of the damage was minimized. In comparison, Typhoon Thelma, which hit southern Taiwan, was far more destructive. When the weather bureau issued a special warning about gusty winds and torrential rainfall, the sky was still completely clear. Consequently, people in southern Taiwan paid little attention and took no precautions against the typhoon. Some even took advantage of the "typhoon holiday" to go traveling. No one thought that this tranquillity was the calm before the storm.

Without any mountain ranges to sap the force of a storm, southern Taiwan is in fact very vulnerable when typhoons strike from the south, which was exactly what Thelma did. The gale sent trees and broken shop signs flying through the air. Many parts of the cities were submerged under seawater, and huge numbers of houses in low-lying areas were flooded. When the storm subsided, many people had been injured and their property damaged. They needed help urgently. Having accumulated much valuable experience in relief work after Typhoon Nara, Tzu Chi members immediately provided aid under the guidance of local government authorities.

Challenge

As soon as the typhoon left Taiwan, Tzu Chi volunteers in southern Taiwan hurried to the Pingtung County household registration office to ask for a list of names of typhoon victims. Only with a list of victims could efficient relief work commence. After waiting in the office for a long time, Tzu Chi members were told by an official to come back in the afternoon, as the list was not yet ready. When the volunteers returned that afternoon, the list was still not ready and they were asked to come again the following morning. The Tzu Chi people became upset, since they believed that offering help to victims was something that could not be delayed. Without a list of names, however, they could do nothing but wait patiently. They returned to the registration office early the following morning, but once again the whole day was wasted.

Some Tzu Chi volunteers could no longer hold back their anger at the inefficiency and indifference of the local officials. They had come to help with the relief work, but the officials seemed ungrateful and unhappy with their "trouble-making."

The news of the bureaucratic inefficiency along with the Tzu Chi members' complaints finally reached Master Cheng Yen in eastern Taiwan.

With a sigh, the Master reminded her followers: "Keep in mind that we are there to carry out relief work, which cannot be done without the assistance of local officials. By volunteering to help, we did in fact increase the workload of the officials. We should not expect to be served, since we are there to serve. Try to foster good relationships with others first, and then we can carry out our work more smoothly."

The Master's words immediately calmed everyone's frustration. Many of the volunteers had to ask themselves whether they were there to help the victims or to receive gratitude for themselves. Since the answer was very clear, they did not give up. They finally received the list on the third day, and the relief work started as planned.

Effects and Reflections

Master Cheng Yen once asked one of her lay disciples, "When someone is offering help, who should be grateful—the one offering or the one receiving?" The disciple gave what she thought a perfect answer, "Both parties should be mutually thankful."

The Master shook her head, pointing out that the one offering should be grateful to the one being helped. The disciple was puzzled. The Master asked her if helping others made her happy. The disciple nodded her head. "Then who gives you the chance to obtain happiness and peace of mind? Isn't it the one you are trying to help? Therefore, you are the one who should be thankful," the Master explained with a smile.

Tzu Chi members are grateful to aid recipients. Helping

others gives us the chance to offer our help to them and thus gain happiness. In the process of extending help we may encounter less-friendly people. When that happens, we must be understanding. The officials assembling the lists of names after Typhoon Thelma saw aiding the disaster's victims as an added burden to their already heavy workload. We should let these officials share in the joy of helping others by warmly praising their cooperation and treating them with respect and understanding.

If we have a condescending attitude while offering help to the needy, they will probably feel uncomfortable. If our motive is truly one of kindness and love, then we will just put our innate respect and care for others into practice by giving help to the needy. It is in fact a way to purify our human nature. Only when we understand the essence of "helping without asking for anything in return" can we truly taste the sweetness of helping others.

Two American psychiatrists in a mental hospital in Boston, Massachusetts, once did a test. They found out that when patients in party A reached out friendly hands to patients in party B, 73 percent of the patients in party B responded in an equally friendly manner. However, 16 percent of the patients in party B responded with hostility because they sensed a tinge of indifference in party A's patients. The study illustrates the Master's teaching that nurturing good relationships with others will always facilitate the task of helping the needy. "Good will induces reciprocal good will, whereas indifference invites reciprocal indifference." It is truly food for thought.

The relief work in the aftermath of Typhoon Thelma taught Tzu Chi members to be grateful not only to the victims, but to everyone involved in the relief tasks, including government officials and members of other charity organizations. It has become an important motto for all Tzu Chi relief efforts ever since then—to do good deeds, we must first nurture good relationships with others.

6 } *Building a self-sufficient organization*

CHALLENGE: Can an organization function without a leader?

"Physical life is impermanent, but wisdom life is everlasting.
The establishment of the Tzu Chi Hospital will prolong
the wisdom life of Tzu Chi like an ever-flowing spring."
MASTER CHENG YEN

Background

At the age of forty-two, Master Cheng Yen suffered a severe bout
of angina pectoris. One night, she awoke with a sudden acute
chest pain. The Master groped around for her medicine but failed
to find it in the darkness. She fainted with the pain and did not
regain consciousness until dawn.

After this scare, the Master realized that the chest pain could
strike at anytime, and that the disease could lead to heart attacks
and even death. "Death is a natural course of life," she reflected,
"but what will happen to the two thousand Tzu Chi aid recipients
if I suddenly die?" To ensure ongoing care for the needy, Master
Cheng Yen decided to find a way to guarantee that the Tzu Chi
missions would continue even after she was gone.

Challenge

The Master contemplated deeply. One day she asked her disciples how they would carry on the Tzu Chi missions after she

passed away. They assured the Master that they would follow her wholeheartedly as long as she was there to lead them. "But after that," they added, "we would simply let nature take its course." The Master nodded. Their answer revealed the core of her concern: while she was alive, her disciples were willing to follow her in doing good deeds, but they would probably stop once she died.

The nuns in the Abode of Still Thoughts were working extremely hard to make a living. They did not have much money left over to finance charity work, and the Master realized that the Tzu Chi Foundation, like a stream without a source, would dry up sooner or later without stable funds to carry out its aid work. The Master therefore decided to search for a spring, an ongoing source of revenue, which would continuously supply the stream, the charitable work for the needy. That wellspring should not only wash away people's pain but also be financially self-sufficient.

The Master fully understood that sickness leads to poverty, and since there were no fully equipped hospitals in eastern Taiwan to treat seriously ill patients, many patients lost their lives due to the delay in receiving treatment. In the summer of 1979, she raised the idea of constructing the biggest, most sophisticated, and most fully equipped hospital in eastern Taiwan. The hospital would carry out Tzu Chi's mission of saving people and helping the poor. And the work should continue even if the Master passed away. She believed that her followers would carry on even after her death and that they would continue raising money to operate these hospitals.

Master Cheng Yen is a person of action. Once the idea was firm in her mind, she was committed to making it happen.

Effects and Reflections
As the membership and the scope of the Tzu Chi Foundation grew, Master Cheng Yen wondered, "When the host of a show

leaves the stage, does the curtain have to fall?" Her solution to the questions of growth and succession was to design a strategy that would allow the foundation to operate without a single leader. In the language of business, the Master "re-engineered" the organization. Instead of seeking to improve the current conditions, the Master set out to solve the problems of the future. The moment she started to talk about building a hospital, Tzu Chi underwent a metamorphosis. That is, according to *Harvard Business Review*, she "created a new framework, leading everyone to embrace an impossible future." Time has proved that the Master successfully "re-engineered" Tzu Chi.

Transformation begins with individuals. We will all die, but before that happens everyone has the responsibility to make the world a better place in which to live. Maybe not everyone is capable of carrying out large-scale philanthropy, but everyone can plant an invisible field of goodness inside themselves. When we sow, spread, and pass on the seeds of goodness, love will pass down from one generation to the next. With determination and confidence, we can all re-engineer ourselves.

two

GROWING PAINS

7 } *Opposition to building a hospital*

CHALLENGE: How does one overcome opposition
and seemingly insurmountable obstacles?

"People with ideals should walk steadfastly
and resolutely, not forcefully, toward their
goal. They will reach it eventually."
MASTER CHENG YEN

Background

When Master Cheng Yen announced to a meeting of her core
disciples her grand hope of building a hospital, she met vehe-
ment opposition from almost everyone. Only one commissioner,
Lin Pi-yu, openly seconded the Master's idea. After the meeting
was over, she immediately reassured the Master that setting up a
hospital was by no means difficult—all they needed to do was to
build several wards, hire some doctors, and buy some basic medical equipment. The Master immediately clarified that she did not
envision a small hospital run by a handful of physicians, but a
general hospital with seven or eight hundred beds and teams of
specialists.

Although Ms. Lin was surprised, she nevertheless admired the
Master's great courage and ambition to help the needy.

Challenge

Why did the disciples and followers, who usually supported the Master, so strongly oppose her idea this time? Most disciples certainly knew it was a worthy venture to build a hospital, but they also felt that such a task was too big a challenge for a small-scale charity association like Tzu Chi. After all, a professional institution like a hospital requires many specific skills and a great deal of knowledge and experience to operate. It is not a business that a few nuns and laypeople could run, especially not with Tzu Chi's meager funds and membership already stretched thin. Many members held that Tzu Chi's charity work was equally meaningful and entirely enough to keep them busy. Their arguments were not groundless. In short, many people tried to dissuade the Master from putting her idea into practice, as she had neither money nor a suitable piece of land on which to build the hospital.

How does one rebut other people's rejections and arguments when they are valid and rational? How does one make the impossible and the overwhelming seem doable, even desirable? Five years after the plan was announced, Tzu Chi members had raised US$750,000 in donations, which amounted to less than 5 percent of the estimated cost of the hospital. That figure hinted that maybe Tzu Chi really did lack the ability to complete such a project.

Yet Master Cheng Yen's decision to build a hospital was based not on the feasibility of the project, but on its necessity. She had the stubborn spirit of the Chinese saying, "No matter how many people oppose me, I will do it." Her unwavering belief that the eastern coast of Taiwan needed a well-established general hospital and that Tzu Chi needed a larger purpose to ensure its vitality, plus her selfless spirit and unflinching determination despite her own frail health, touched many members. They began to set aside their own reservations to support the Master and her vision. And because her health was uncertain, the members began to see the project as a race against time. Their wholehearted devotion brought out hidden potential in themselves, and with the concerted efforts of so many people, they began to accomplish what many had thought to be impossible.

Effects and Reflections

If the Master had taken her disciples' advice and given up her strength of vision, then Tzu Chi might well have remained a small religious charity group in Hualien.

However, the Master seems to continuously challenge the impossible, attempting things most people see as beyond her ability to cope with. Yet, with her passion, determination, and selfless dedication, she has surmounted all these difficulties and achieved the seemingly unachievable. In doing so, she has inspired many people to join her.

Throughout history, figures such as Jesus Christ, the Buddha, and Mother Teresa, who had neither power nor money nor good health, did what their contemporaries deemed impossible—with their endurance, love for peace, and complete dedication. Similarly, the Master is determined to overcome all adversities and misunderstandings to relieve anyone from suffering. Wherever there are calls for help, she will extend her hands. Time and again under her leadership, Tzu Chi people create inspiring miracles of love, even in areas that are completely unfamiliar to them.

8 } *Raising money one donor at a time*

CHALLENGE: When should one turn down $200 million?

"The field of blessings should be cultivated by all. It's
people's hearts, not money, that Tzu Chi wants to raise."
MASTER CHENG YEN

Background
After the news about Tzu Chi's hospital plan and its fundraising
efforts was published in media reports and in the foundation's
monthly magazine, which was written by commissioners and
distributed through local offices, many good-hearted people
responded. However, the US$20 million that was estimated for
the construction of the hospital seemed to be beyond reach.

In 1981, during a national meeting of Tzu Chi commissioners,
one devoted commissioner from southern Taiwan had some good
news: "A Japanese friend is willing to donate US$200 million for
the hospital construction." The Master was surprised and asked
why this friend would make such a generous donation.

The Japanese man was a Buddhist and had been brought up
in Hualien, Taiwan, during the Japanese occupation of 1895–
1945. In return for the late President Chiang Kai-shek allowing
the defeated Japanese to return to their homeland at the end of
World War II, this man wanted to do something for Taiwan. The

commissioners were delighted by the news of the $200 million donation, which would go a long way toward helping Tzu Chi reach its goal.

Challenge

The commissioners were excited by this large donation, but Master Cheng Yen said, "Obviously $200 million is very tempting, but we will have to decline." The commissioners were dumbfounded. "Why?" they asked.

The Master calmly gave them three reasons. First, given Taiwan's prosperous economy, the citizens should be able to build the hospital with their own resources. She hoped the Taiwanese people could cultivate this field of blessings and then enjoy the results once it was completed. Second, major investors might expect to have the final say in policy-making with respect to business operations, and concentrating operational control in the hands of a few people ran counter to the Master's original ideal. The Master felt that to avoid any future conflict between major donors and Tzu Chi in running the hospital, it would be best to decline such large offers. The last and the most important reason was that the Master intended to set up the hospital through the united effort and love of many people, so that it would be a hospital for everyone. "Merits are to be cultivated by all," she proclaimed. "The seeds of blessings are to be planted by all."

Effects and Reflections

The Master's clarity and strength of vision motivated Tzu Chi members to work even harder to raise funds. Many of them went from door to door, day and night, talking about the Master's compassionate vow to build a hospital. A sizable fund was raised, and many touching events took place along the way. The Master often said: "The amount of a donation is not important. What is important is to bring out kindness and compassion in others."

Helping people to help themselves is one of the principles behind Robert Pamplin Jr.'s philanthropy. One of the four hundred richest people in the world, according to *Forbes* magazine, and chairman of the boards of three colleges in the United States, he is well-known for his charity work. In 1992, Mr. Pamplin offered to donate US$250,000 to Lewis & Clark College in the name of anyone who matched or outdid him in push-ups, sit-ups, pull-ups, or rope climbing. Their names were also to be engraved in the library in memory of this event. Instead of simply giving US$1 million to the library, Mr. Pamplin reasoned, this contest would inspire people to get involved. In the future, participants could visit the college with their children or grandchildren and say, "Look, I helped raise money for this library!" The fundraising was a huge success.

Mr. Pamplin's way of carrying out charity work and the Master's method of funding hospitals and schools show how effectively people work together when they can see the results of their efforts. In this way, they develop a sense of responsibility and pride toward their community.

9 } *Securing land to save lives*

CHALLENGE: When is it important to
fight and when is it better to give in?

"To give is to receive. To make things easier
for others is the best way to help oneself."
MASTER CHENG YEN

Background

Finding a site suitable for the hospital proved to be more difficult
than people had originally thought. For the first year and four
months, each day was spent searching for the proper site. Every
possible site was looked into. Altogether, the Master considered
eight possible pieces of land, but unfortunately, because of size
and zoning problems, none of the potential sites could be used.

In 1980, Lin Yang-kang, then governor of Taiwan Province,
visited the Abode of Still Thoughts, where the Master lived. He
was amazed when he saw the nuns tending the fields and busily
making handicrafts. Having the impression that Buddhist monks
and nuns simply lived off offerings made by their followers, he
asked the Master in bewilderment, "Do you work, too?"

While giving a tour around the shabbily furnished Abode,
the Master briefed Governor Lin on the hospital plans and the
difficulties in finding a suitable piece of land. The Master's

commitment touched Governor Lin, and he promised to help in land acquisition.

When he returned to Taipei, Governor Lin immediately reported to then President Chiang Ching-kuo about the work of Master Cheng Yen and the Tzu Chi Foundation. Three days later, President Chiang himself visited the Abode. All Tzu Chi members were excited and encouraged by this unprecedented event. After President Chiang's visit, "important people" paid visits to the Abode, one after another, to see it with their own eyes. It seemed that a suitable piece of land might soon be made available.

As expected, within the next six months, Governor Lin offered Tzu Chi a piece of land by Meilun River in Hualien. The paperwork took a year to complete, but Tzu Chi finally had a piece of land—four years after the plan was first announced. On February 5, 1983, Tzu Chi held the groundbreaking ceremony for its hospital. Although it was a rainy day, everyone who attended was beaming.

Challenge

Just as the Master's long-awaited dream was about to be realized came the shocking news that the military wanted to reclaim the land to construct an air base. Work on the hospital had to be halted immediately. For many days and many nights, the Master could not eat or sleep.

Residents living adjacent to the land were also upset, because once an air base was built the value of their properties would plummet. As a result, the local residents approached the Master and asked her to appeal to the authorities. They even promised to donate more land to Tzu Chi if the Master would agree to fight for them.

As tempting and beneficial for both parties as this offer seemed, the Master declined it. She concluded, "As citizens of this country, we should regard national defense as a top priority. The military must have its reason for using this piece of land and we should not interfere with its project." The land was gone and all the hard work of securing it seemed to have been in vain.

Effects and Reflections

Upon hearing the news, Lin Yang-kang, who had since taken the position of interior minister, called and comforted the Master: "Master, maybe the bodhisattvas are not pleased with that piece of land, or maybe they are testing your faith. As long as you are persistent and determined, I'm sure the bodhisattvas will help you find a better piece of land." Minister Lin then called Chief of General Staff Soong Chang-chih and explained that Tzu Chi's hospital project had been halted by the military's decision to build a base at Hualien. Admiral Soong was deeply impressed with the Master's position, putting national defense above all else, and promised to look into the matter. Soon after, incumbent Governor Lee Teng-hui learned about the situation and immediately set up a task force to assist Tzu Chi in finding another piece of land.

Many things in the world are obtained by giving, not fighting. As Lao Tzu, one of the wisest philosophers in ancient China, said, "The more you help others, the more you gain. The more you give to others, the more you receive." The Master's decision clearly shows that to be true.

10 } *The decision to return donations*

CHALLENGE: Should money intended
for one purpose be used for another?

"The one and only way to give others and
ourselves peace of mind is to always act
with sincerity, integrity, and trust."
MASTER CHENG YEN

Background

Despite all the hard work put into finding the tract of land for
building the hospital and the fact that the official groundbreaking ceremony had already been held, the construction project was
back at square one. No one was sure when and where the hospital
would be built. The Master faced another test: what to do with
the hospital funds raised over the previous years?

The Master shut herself in a room and knelt in front of a
statue of Kuan Yin Bodhisattva. After many days of pondering
without eating, drinking, or sleeping, the Master concluded that
no matter how upset she felt, she must lift her spirits so that her
followers would not worry about her. At that moment, she also
decided that she must return every dollar of the money raised for
the hospital to the donors.

Challenge

It is almost unprecedented for a religious organization to return money to its donors. Many people believe that religious organizations have the right to manage the donations they receive; therefore, even though Tzu Chi's hospital might not be built, many members felt the money could still be used for other projects.

Master Cheng Yen, however, insists that donations raised for a specific purpose can be used only for that purpose. Therefore, she reasoned, any money meant to help Tzu Chi build a hospital should certainly be returned. Without each donor's consent, the funds could not be used for other purposes. The Master explained, "We have a detailed record of each donation. Therefore, reimbursement shouldn't be too difficult."

Effects and Reflections

Master Cheng Yen repeatedly asks all Tzu Chi members to act with sincerity, integrity, and trust. Each donation is recorded according to its specific purpose, and because of such accountability, the Tzu Chi Foundation is well trusted by the public.

Tzu Chi members offer help, not handouts, to the needy. The Master strictly requires that all materials be distributed with sincerity and respect, and that they be well packaged. Thus used clothes to be handed out must not be dirty, tattered, or sloppily wrapped. Instead they must be clean and wrapped nicely so that the recipients may feel happy and respected. "What you do not want for yourself you must not give to others," she says. You should always have a respectful manner when helping others. Put yourself in their shoes and ask yourself if you would like to receive ragged junk in the name of charity.

Similarly, during one of the early rice distributions to Tzu

Chi's aid recipients at the Abode of Still Thoughts, some grains of rice fell out of holes in a few of the bags. A member picked up the grains one by one and added them to the vat of rice cooking at the Abode. A nun saw this and spoke to the member: "I know you don't want to see the rice go to waste, but we shouldn't keep the rice in our own vat, because every grain was donated by some kind person for the poor." This is one example of how the Master and her disciples thoroughly live up to the principles of sincerity, integrity, and trust.

When the Master decided to live up to her principles by returning the money to each donor, who could have predicted that this gesture would become a turning point for Tzu Chi's hospital project?

11 } *Investing in the future*

CHALLENGE: When is it better to put off a
short-term need in favor of long-term security?

"In making decisions, one should not only assess the present,
but also future conditions, to avoid leaving problems for the
next person to deal with." MASTER CHENG YEN

Background

After returning the seven hectares (17 acres) of land in the sub-
urbs of Hualien so the military could build its air base, Tzu Chi
was later offered nine hectares (22 acres) of easily accessible land
close to the center of the city. The Master's compassion, courage,
determination, and most of all her integrity made a formidable
impression on Interior Minister Lin Yang-kang, and she received
more assistance from the military and the government. When
Tzu Chi submitted the application to acquire and use the new
plot of land, the paperwork was completed and approved in no
time. The bigger size and better location, however, meant the cost
of the land was much higher. Tzu Chi was to face another challenge, given its tight budget.

Provincial Governor Lee Teng-hui, who had made this new
piece of land available, was aware of Tzu Chi's financial problem.
He thought it would be a shame if the hospital plan failed due to

the high land price. After careful consideration, he came up with a brilliant proposal: the government would lease the land to Tzu Chi for just one dollar.

Challenge

Despite the fact that leasing the land rather than purchasing it would leave Tzu Chi money to buy hospital equipment and hire prominent physicians, the Master thanked Governor Lee for his "one-dollar" goodwill, but insisted on purchasing the land. She asked only that the government sell the land to Tzu Chi at a favorable price.

Given Tzu Chi's strapped financial situation, her decision was baffling both to her disciples and to Governor Lee. They could not understand the Master's decision, unless it was to save her pride. She explained to Governor Lee that although she was grateful for his kind offer, she knew that people and situations change. Sooner or later, he would be promoted from his current position and the Master might no longer be around. Later, then, the governor's kind proposal might turn out to be problematic. She believed it was best to buy the land as soon as possible.

Effects and Reflections

Just as the Master had predicted, Governor Lee was promoted. It is difficult to know whether his successors in the provincial governor's office would have unconditionally maintained his rental agreement with Tzu Chi.

Furthermore, the value of land has skyrocketed. If Tzu Chi had leased the land for a dollar, it would surely have led to protests from local residents, landowners, and even city councilors who were paying more for their land. And it might have required that government officials and Tzu Chi members renegotiate the arrangement. If Tzu Chi had then wanted to lease or buy the land at the market price, it would have been a tremendous financial burden. Looking at all these possible outcomes, one has to admire the Master's foresight. To the Master, no decision should endanger the continuity of the hospital or cause problems for people to deal with in the future.

Many decision-makers only look to solve existing dilemmas or situations without looking ahead and pondering potential problems. If one always considers the future carefully, the chance of paying a high price for a wrong decision will be minimized.

Competing for the Future, a book by Gary Hamel and C.K. Prahalad about how businesses can stay competitive, emphasizes that foresight is a prerequisite to success. It also points out that to cultivate this foresight, one should develop the "imaginary ability" to predict the outcomes of events before they happen. The Master's ability to imagine future outcomes stems from her thorough understanding of the impermanent nature of all things, her belief in not seeking the easy solution, and her attitude of always thinking about others. In fact, these three motivations can be seen in all the Master's major decisions.

12 } *An army of fundraisers can make a difference*

CHALLENGE: How can one person inspire
others toward a common goal?

"One's strength is as great as one's commitment."
MASTER CHENG YEN

Background

Once the Master had obtained the new tract of land for the
hospital, fundraising efforts could begin again. Tzu Chi members, having seen the Master's commitment to this project, were
spurred to gather the US$20 million needed as fast as possible.

Tzu Chi members had previously raised and then returned
US$750,000. At such a slow pace they realized it would take
more than fifty years to raise all the money. Resolved to have the
hospital built as soon as possible, Tzu Chi members doubled their
efforts, trying all different ways to raise funds. As the Chinese
saying goes, "Tiny grains of sand can pile up to make a pagoda."

Challenge

Raising funds is the most challenging task for many nonprofit
and charity organizations. They design attention-grabbing fundraisers and eye-catching slogans, and they solicit donations from
the media, businesses, and the government. Yet for Tzu Chi, such

flashy methods and resource-pooling abilities were out of reach. However, they knew that good organization would help them realize their objectives more quickly.

The thousands of Tzu Chi commissioners living across Taiwan provided the foundation with a perfect fundraising network. The organization's meticulous recording of every donation had won it high credibility among local people and the trust of many donors. Now commissioners worked harder than ever. They went from door to door, soliciting funds by expounding the Master's idea of doing good deeds and explaining why she aspired to build a hospital. Their dedication paid off. People responded positively; in fact, one commissioner raised over half a million dollars in only a few months. Other Tzu Chi members took on additional work as janitors and dishwashers and donated every penny they earned to the hospital construction fund.

The Master believes that the Buddha's teachings should be practiced through action, not just through talking, so she rarely gives public lectures. However, for the sake of fundraising for the hospital, she gave lectures on sutras in Tzu Chi's Taipei office every month for three years and she traveled around the island promoting Buddhism. Moved by her determination and kindness, many people donated generously. The funds for building the hospital accumulated rapidly.

Tzu Chi also held large-scale fundraising activities. At the first charity bazaar in Taipei in 1983, the number of participants and the amount of support were unprecedented in Taiwan's history. Many people bought items at auction, then donated these items so that they could be auctioned again to raise more money. The following year, the wife of General Sun Li-jen donated all her gold ornaments and jewels to the charity auction. Although she was a celebrity, she dressed plainly at the bazaar. "I've donated all the valuables I have," she told the Master. "If I'm blessed enough to own more jewelry in the future, I will keep donating everything to Tzu Chi." Her words deeply moved everyone present. Other members of the public gave their lifetime savings, their houses, their inheritances, and their title deeds for land. Tzu Chi was a relatively unknown organization, so this altruism was truly precious.

To recognize these generous contributions and to encourage the public to share what they had with the less fortunate in our society, Tzu Chi's Honorary Board member system was established. Anyone who donated US$25,000 became a member of the Tzu Chi Honorary Board, a title without any substantial privileges. However, many people responded warmly to the Master's call to donate such a sum because they not only saw it as an honor to participate, but they also understood the urgency of the construction project.

With their concerted, relentless efforts, Tzu Chi people successfully reached the target of $20 million ahead of schedule.

Effects and Reflections

One drop of water evaporates quickly without a trace, but an infinite number of drops will converge into a river nourishing life on Earth. An individual's effort, as small as a drop of water, might not raise $20 million, but the accumulated effort of ten thousand, one hundred thousand or even one million individuals definitely can.

The Master reminded her disciples that confidence is essential in undertaking any task: she had strong belief in her own selflessness and she had confidence that everyone had love in their hearts. First, she knew that she did not want to achieve her own ends by setting up the hospital; therefore, she was confident of raising the necessary funds. Secondly, she believed that what she did would win other loving people's support and endorsement, so that they would surely respond to her calls to do good deeds.

Finding the right method is also vital in realizing one's purpose. Tzu Chi used fundraisers, lectures on Buddhism, and its Honorary Board member system to appeal for public participation and to bring out everyone's innate potential. The Master knew that because of the foundation's trustworthiness, people would respond positively to Tzu Chi's call and that its members would continue to offer their selfless devotion. The Master's wisdom, confidence, persistence, encouragement, and trust in all Tzu Chi members helped them to believe in themselves and their ability to reach this goal. As the Master often says, "Our strength is as great as our commitment." When the enthusiasm for the seemingly unrealistic hospital construction project reached a certain point, it suddenly became possible.

Social scientists have pointed out that the success of an endeavor lies not solely in one's ability, but more importantly in one's self-confidence. Such confidence comes from the single-minded, unwavering effort to accomplish the tasks that one believes in and relates to. This self-confidence will be strengthened if one keeps receiving encouragement from others.

The Master hopes that those who join Tzu Chi will find meaning and direction in life not through fame and wealth, but by thoroughly understanding Tzu Chi's true ideals and spirit. She hopes that Tzu Chi members can create a world of love by working together and doing good deeds. She often tells those who are interested in Tzu Chi not to rush into donating money. "I would like them to spend some time observing and getting to know Tzu

Chi first," she explains. Only when one is truly touched by the ideals of an institution can one identify oneself completely with it and make one's most significant contributions.

13 } *Attracting top staff to the hospital*

CHALLENGE: How does one dispel doubts
when doing something for the first time?

"With humility, compassion, and trust, one can surmount
all difficulties and achieve any task." MASTER CHENG YEN

Background

Could a group of nuns and homemakers run a highly specialized
hospital? The public certainly had their doubts about the management of the hospital. Given the fact that Tzu Chi members lacked
hospital management knowledge and experience, such skepticism
was understandable. What tricks did Master Cheng Yen use to
ensure that the Hualien Tzu Chi General Hospital would survive,
even thrive?

Aware of how little she knew about hospital management, the
Master visited quite a few hospitals and humbly asked the staff to
share their experiences of success as well as failure. She believed
that understanding the elements leading to success was of great
value, but that looking at the factors leading to failure deserved
much more attention, as this information could help her avoid
making the same mistakes. Moreover, considering the donors'
expectations of the fledgling Tzu Chi Hospital, she felt she could
not afford to stumble, not even once.

Challenge

Studying the failure of a hospital in southern Taiwan taught the Master an especially important lesson: the absolute necessity to find competent doctors. She began searching for suitable medical staff the moment construction commenced. To make Tzu Chi Hospital a first-class organization, she targeted the best doctors. Although Tzu Chi could not offer handsome salaries, the Master firmly believed that conscientious physicians would be attracted and recruited by the hospital's noble ideal of serving the poor and needy.

She eagerly sought cooperation with the National Taiwan University Hospital (NTUH), which has always been regarded as one of the leading hospitals in Taiwan. At her invitation, senior doctors from NTUH agreed to treat outpatients at the Tzu Chi Hospital once a week, and the university's medical students could choose to intern at the new hospital. Such arrangements would enable the foundation to provide good-quality services usually available only at large hospitals. Before long, she hoped, the hospital would build up a reputation for reliability in eastern Taiwan.

The Master also realized that the ability and professionalism of the leadership could have a decisive influence on the future of any newly established institution. Dr. Tu Shih-mien and Dr. Tseng Wen-ping, the deputy superintendents of NTUH, were moved by the Master's dedication to the ideal of Tzu Chi Hospital. They agreed to take the positions of first and second superintendent of Tzu Chi Hospital. Both men helped Tzu Chi with its construction planning even before the ground was first broken, so they well knew the Master's high hopes for the hospital and her respect for professionals. The Master's choice was the right one. The expertise and strong medical ethics of the two superintendents not only laid a good foundation for the Tzu Chi Hospital, but also facilitated cooperation with other renowned hospitals.

As deputy superintendent of NTUH, Dr. Tu had been busy, but his care for each patient and for medical development in Taiwan never wavered. He made time to give his professional advice on the construction of Tzu Chi Hospital in over a hundred preparatory meetings. So, many people were shocked to learn that he had been diagnosed with liver cancer and was told he had three more months to live. Despite Dr. Tu's health condition, the Master did not change her decision to invite him to serve as the Tzu Chi Hospital's superintendent. When Dr. Tu asked the Master why, she replied with a smile, "My own heart condition is also a ticking bomb that might explode at any minute." So these two people, each harboring a disease, worked together to build an ideal hospital for people living in eastern Taiwan.

Even though the Master knew Dr. Tu's days were numbered, why did she ask him to shoulder this heavy responsibility? The reasons were simple: she trusted his expertise and, most important of all, she believed that because of his fatal disease, Superintendent Tu would be able to empathize with his patients more than ever and know the importance of respecting and making the best use of life.

The Master's full cooperation with, confidence in, and respect for Superintendent Tu gave him a free hand in running the hospital. With the reciprocity of love and a strong sense of accomplishment, Dr. Tu successfully suppressed his cancer and carved out a bright future for the hospital.

Effects and Reflections
Working in one's area of expertise is definitely easier than working

in a brand new field. However, some people can successfully run a business they know very little about. The key to success, I believe, is for nonprofessional managers to grasp the main principles of policy-making and delegate the implementation to specialists. As long as nonprofessional managers trust and authorize their employees to make decisions, then very likely they will do an outstanding job.

Yeh Kuang-shih, dean of the Institute of Communication Management of the National Sun Yat-sen University, stated in his article "From Nonprofessional to Professional" that the boss of a company needs two traits: entrepreneurial knowledge and managerial ability. He points out that in an established company a new boss should give precedence to managerial ability: "The lack of experience or preset bias toward the new work actually grants them the vision and courage of creativity." A new manager certainly needs assistance from professionals at the same time.

Often, company managers lament how hard it is to find the right staff. However, medical professionals and volunteers willingly provide their assistance to the Tzu Chi Hospital because they feel Master Cheng Yen respects and trusts them. They can sense her sincerity, and they believe in Tzu Chi because of the merits and credibility that the organization has accumulated throughout the years. The Master believes that if we can firmly uphold our principles and can convince others that what we strive for is truly beneficial to our society, then talent will naturally come to us.

14 } *Determining the number of beds*

CHALLENGE: How does one find a
balance between ideals and reality?

"Finding the delicate point of balance between
flexibility and persistence is an art. We should be
flexible in our approach by listening to others'
opinions, but be persistent in upholding our ideals."
MASTER CHENG YEN

Background

The number of beds determines the capacity of a hospital. The
experts on the committee unanimously concluded that two hundred beds would be best. But this figure was far lower than the
Master had envisioned. According to her calculations, the hospital
should have at least five hundred beds in order to serve patients in
eastern Taiwan. The more beds, the more suffering patients can
be saved—this was Master Cheng Yen's ideal. However, the professionals on the construction committee reminded the Master of
the reality: how much "market share" could Tzu Chi have in the
lightly populated Hualien area, which already had the Menno-
nite Christian Hospital, the 803 Army General Hospital, and the
Taiwan Provincial Hualien Hospital? Yet, the hospital that the
Master envisioned was still needed because these three original

hospitals were small in scale and medically less advanced. There were a lot of operations they couldn't perform.

Challenge

Should the Master insist on having five hundred beds or accept the suggested number of two hundred? The choice was apparently difficult, as the Master expressed her anguish to her disciples several times: "I believe that with more beds, the hospital can help more people. But I have no experience in running hospitals. The committee members are professionals in this line of work. Since I invited them to do the planning, I should respect their decisions, rather than imposing my own on them. If the hospital is not full, it would be a waste of our resources and, worst of all, it might even create a serious deficit. I really must take all aspects into consideration."

After mulling over the issue for quite a while, the Master finally came up with a compromise: she agreed to have two hundred beds, but she insisted that the lobby must be the same size as that of a larger hospital, in order to accommodate patients comfortably.

Effects and Reflections

I believe the success of running a hospital lies in teamwork, not in a one-person show led by the Master. Since she had entrusted the hospital planning to medical professionals, she was right to respect and trust their judgment and decisions. The hospital might have been well received by the local community had the Master insisted on five hundred beds, but such a decision might have caused an irrecoverable deficit or provoked a strong sense of alienation or disappointment among the professional managers. What then would Tzu Chi have gained?

The Master's compromise, with the condition of a spacious lobby, ensured room for future expansion. Even if the number of beds was to increase to seven hundred (as it did less than two years later), the lobby would still be capable of accommodating a greater number of patients waiting to register. It was a perfect arrangement. By accepting the experts' suggestion, her relationship with them was maintained. By leaving room for future growth, the problem of expanding the lobby was avoided, and the medical staff was able to envision serving more patients. Thus, everyone was encouraged to work harder.

Tests in environmental psychology show that when people are placed in a crowded environment, they feel pressured, which has a negative impact on their health. A spacious lobby decreases the chances that patients might feel stressed and irritated due to long waiting times, and consequently lowers the chances that patients might sink into even worse health. The Master's consideration was completely in line with her hope to rid people of suffering. For the sake of human health, companies and governments should ensure adequately large open spaces in their plans for construction and city development to allow for future expansion.

15 } *A free clinic for the community*

CHALLENGE: When is a missed deadline an opportunity?

"A hospital is to serve people and a free clinic is a
manifestation of love. They are concrete ways
Tzu Chi practices the Buddha's compassion."
MASTER CHENG YEN

Background
After many unexpected problems and events, the construction of
the long-awaited Buddhist Tzu Chi General Hospital was completed in August 1986, nine months ahead of schedule. The early
completion was both a blessing and a problem. On one hand, the
commitment to serving the needy could be realized earlier than
expected, but on the other hand much of the operating structure
had not yet been established. Most doctors had not yet taken up
their posts at the newly built hospital, the personnel training plan
was not finished, and the administrative staff were unfamiliar
with the work procedures.

Challenge
Master Cheng Yen believed that since the hospital had been completed, it should be utilized to the fullest extent. She pondered
for a long time and finally came up with a solution: the Tzu Chi

Hospital would provide a free clinic for two weeks before its official grand opening. This warm-up activity would give the staff a chance to get used to the hospital and the public the opportunity to seek medical treatment. Her proposal was well received and supported by everyone.

At 7:30 a.m. on August 3, 1986, in the 670-square-meter (7,200-sq-ft) hospital foyer, a simple ceremony was held to mark the beginning of the free clinic. The Master told those present that every brick and every grain of sand bore the love of all kindhearted supporters of Tzu Chi. Tzu Chi members always carry out the Buddha's compassion through concrete actions, and the Master reminded everyone, "This hospital was built to serve, and now we want to bring love to the needy by holding this free clinic."

After the thirty-minute ceremony, the free clinic commenced. Over a thousand people registered to be treated on the first day. Within the first two weeks, the free clinic treated 7,400 patients at a total cost of over US$92,000.

All the hard work the medical staff put in and all the money spent were worthwhile. The staff became familiar with the new environment, and the patients at the free clinic were overwhelmingly grateful.

Effects and Reflections

Moving up a deadline is not a challenge unique to Tzu Chi—many companies have also had such an experience. Rushed procedures and inadequate preparations undoubtedly provoke many complaints from both employees and clients. Yet putting off the opening date adds to the company's expenses, wastes resources, and above all reduces team spirit among employees. Obviously, both options have their disadvantages, so the Master's alternative, the two-week free clinic, helped bring the hospital's opening date nearer, as well as assisting many local residents and promoting the ideals of the Tzu Chi Hospital to them.

Free service has become a strategy that many stores use to attract potential buyers. This approach can kill two birds with one stone: the free service often provides good publicity, and the problems pointed out by customers can help the company improve its service. We could say that the Tzu Chi Hospital was the forerunner of such free service in Taiwan.

The Master decided to hold the free clinic for more than just commercial reasons. The hospital was built on the selfless giving of many supporters, and to honor this commitment the Master feels that no resources should be left idle—be they time, people, or materials. She also feels that the needs and feelings of the patients, easy accessibility, and competent medical care, as well as team spirit among the medical staff, are of equal importance. The free clinic would serve as a training opportunity, enabling the medical staff to develop the most suitable working procedures. Since treating patients is the priority of the Tzu Chi Hospital—and these clinics, which serve the needy without charge, carry out that spirit—Tzu Chi continues to hold regular free clinics.

Because of her wholehearted devotion, the Master showed that a good solution will come to those who ponder the problem carefully. Most importantly, the method must be consistent with the objective, lest expedient means damage the original ideal and the fundamental purpose.

16 } *Creating a loving hospital*

CHALLENGE: How does one put
Buddhist principles into action?

"Doctors should not only treat patients' illnesses,
but look after their psychological needs as well."
MASTER CHENG YEN

Background

After the grand opening, the management of the Hualien Tzu Chi
General Hospital gradually got up to speed. The challenge now
was to incorporate Buddhist principles, so the hospital could dis-
tinguish itself from other medical institutions. How could this be
achieved? Should the administrators employ personnel with Buddhist backgrounds or request that the patients study Buddhism?

Challenge

The Master does not employ staff based on religious considerations. Hospital physicians include Protestants and Catholics, as
well as atheists. In fact, the idea of asking all patients and staff
members to read Buddhist scriptures never occurred to the Master.
She believes that a genuine Buddhist hospital should put the Buddha's teachings into practice. The Buddha came to the world to
redeem all living beings from their suffering; thus, the first thing

the Master did was to make saving patients at any cost the hospital's top priority.

The Master made it clear that unlike other hospitals, the Tzu Chi Hospital would not require any deposit and that anyone who needed care should receive it.

The Master gave an inspiring speech to the doctors just after the hospital opened. She said solemnly: "Doctors, you are not here to cure illness." Her words baffled everyone. If a doctor's job was not to treat diseases, then what was it? The Master continued, "You are here to treat patients as human beings, and not merely as cases. Please remember to take care of their psychological as well as their physical needs."

In the foyer of the hospital, there is an eight-meter-high (26-ft) mural entitled *The Buddha Cares for the Sick*, depicting a story of the Buddha. Over two thousand years ago, there was a monk who focused all his attention on his spiritual cultivation and seldom made friends. When others fell sick, he was indifferent and unsympathetic since he did not consider it his business. One day, he himself became seriously ill. When he cried for help, nobody came to his aid. His wounds became ulcerated and he smelled awful.

When the Buddha heard what had happened, he went with a group of monks to see him. A foul odor greeted them as they approached the house. The disciples turned aside and covered their noses with their hands, but the Buddha walked straight up to the monk without the least hesitation. Lifting the old man's robes slightly, the Buddha found that the man's body was covered with abscesses. Urine and feces covered the floor. The Buddha asked his disciples to fetch some water, and then he bent down to bathe the monk and dress his sores. He said to him, "According to the law of cause and effect, you reap what you sow. You didn't offer your love to others in the past, so of course you can receive no concern from others now. One should constantly cultivate a loving heart filled with compassion. Cultivating your own spirituality is certainly a meritorious deed, but it is more important to put what you have learned into practice. The greatest merit lies in helping to relieve the suffering of the sick." The monk received enlightenment then and there.

This mosaic mural by the great painter Yen Shui-lung brings to life the compassion of the Buddha. It sends out blessings to all patients and medical staff who walk by. It also illustrates the ideal of this hospital—to respect all life.

The Buddha is known as the Great Healer. The Master often says that all doctors are conscientious Great Healers who uphold medical ethics. To patients, doctors are like living buddhas, so doctors should look after the physical and psychological illnesses of their patients. In Taiwan, people often call nurses "angels in white." The Master calls them "white-clad Kuan Yin Bodhisattvas." (In Taiwan, Kuan Yin is often portrayed as a woman dressed in a white robe who answers all cries for help.) These names recognize the critical value of all medical personnel and give a new interpretation to doctor-patient relations.

Effects and Reflections

Tzu Chi Hospital has been praised for being the first medical institution in Taiwan to waive the security deposit fee. It eventually pushed the national Department of Health to eliminate this inhumane custom, which had been practiced in the country for many decades.

More importantly, the emphasis on "whole person" care (treating the patient's body, mind, and spirit), on seeing the role of doctors and patients as equally valuable, on nurturing conscientious doctors, and on respecting the dignity of each patient have all laid a solid foundation for the hospital. They are the missions of the institution and are surely in line with the essence of Buddhism.

Thus, Tzu Chi Hospital has become a spiritual cultivation ground for all volunteers. Tzu Chi members learn to serve, to humble themselves, to seize each moment, and to be considerate and attentive. Moreover, many people learn the true value of gratitude—to be grateful to the physicians, nurses, and patients for all the opportunities for serving others. In this process, they realize the meaning of life and the importance of giving unselfishly.

Pressures from the heavy workload and the anguish and dejection written on patients' faces occasionally wear the medical personnel down. To support them, the Master formed a Tzu Chi Hospital Volunteer Team to share the work. The most important task of volunteers is to let the doctors and nurses know how much their patients appreciate them, since the patients themselves are often too preoccupied with pain or anxiety to do so. The volunteers, Tzu Chi members from all over Taiwan, also share much of the administrative and general affairs work. Although these members come to the hospital from their hometowns just to do chores for three to seven days, they are always happy. The respect and gratitude they show the medical staff touch the doctors and nurses and raise everyone's spirits and the overall level of care.

Hospital work, just like any work, can sometimes be tiring, tedious, and boring. To add joy to such work, the tasks have meaningful names. All patients are "buddhas" because they show us the suffering in the world and bestow on us the chance to give. The volunteers who visit different patients to deliver medical records are "walking-around buddhas." And those who wash the patients are "bathing buddhas." These inspiring names remind volunteers that they are doing spiritual cultivation in the hospital.

K.E. Appel, a neurological therapist, concluded: "The amiable friendship between doctors and patients is the key element of successful treatment." Many people have commented that the Tzu Chi hospital is a cozy place, that it does not smell like a hospital because the human warmth dilutes the medicinal odors.

17 } *Healing a broken body*

CHALLENGE: How does one nurture
faith in the face of suffering?

"To endure suffering is to eliminate suffering.
We will have new life once we eradicate suffering
and bad karma. You can't escape suffering. If
you can confront, accept, and conquer the challenge
of suffering, you are indeed a winner in life."

MASTER CHENG YEN

Background

Lin Chuan-chin is a member of the aboriginal Bunun tribe in
Taiwan. Because of his family's financial problems, he dropped out
of junior high school and became an apprentice in a nearby garage.
One day in 1987, he and his boss were called to fix a recently
repaired truck that had broken down on a riverbed. They drove
out to the river, and when they arrived, Lin immediately got under
the truck to inspect it. As he did so, the ground beneath the truck
suddenly gave way, sending many tons of marble that had been in
the bed crashing to the ground and pinning Lin underneath the
vehicle. His employer immediately dashed off to find a large crane
or a heavy-duty lifter, but it was three or four hours before Lin was

finally dug out. By the time Lin arrived at the Tzu Chi Hospital nearly five hours after the accident, he was near death, and all the bones in the lower half of his body were completely pulverized.

Challenge

Under the leadership of Dr. Chen Ying-ho, director of the Orthopedics Department, nurses transfused more than 20,000 cc of blood and used more than 6,000 gallons of saline water to clean the gravel from the young man's wounds. Various doctors stabilized the abdominal region, created an artificial anus, reconstructed the organs of the urinary system, connected the hip arteries, amputated the left leg and supported Lin's pelvis with an external frame made of stainless steel. The surgery went on for six hours.

Although he survived the initial surgery, no one could be sure that Lin would be able to endure the follow-up therapy. Shortly after the initial surgery, doctors had to amputate his right leg, as well, due to a severe infection. Not a day went by without more tissue being removed. Many people wondered how, if Lin survived, he was going to live with such an incomplete body.

The Master visited Lin almost every day, constantly encouraging and reminding him: "Look around you; there are a lot more people less fortunate and with less hope. You must have faith and courage. If we strive together, you will live on." The Master also reminded the medical team that Lin had to be saved regardless of the expense. She had faith that he would eventually be healed.

Lin also reassured the Master that he would live on. Even though he had no idea what he could accomplish in the future, he heard the Master's words: "Don't underestimate yourself. Anyone can contribute to society." He also knew that as long as there was life, there was hope.

Six months after the accident, Lin began to exercise his arms, bathe and clean himself, and operate his wheelchair himself. He was able to roam freely around the hospital. A year and a half later, Lin was transferred to National Taiwan University Hospital to receive physical therapy. He began to attend night school at Ming Chuan College, then transferred to an experimental school in Changhua in 1990. He eventually established a multimedia computer studio.

Effects and Reflections

Lin Chuan-chin not only completed his education and acquired professional computer skills, he also participated in regional swimming competitions and won gold medals at some meets in the early nineties.

Lin was a member of Tzu Chi. At the Hualien Tzu Chi General Hospital, he brought food to all the wards, collected lunch boxes, volunteered at the information desk. Visiting patients was one of his most important jobs: he sowed the seeds of love by encouraging patients like himself so that they could emerge from the shadow of despair through the hope that he gave them. He is a living example of what can be accomplished if we don't quit.

Hardship and suffering are unavoidable in life: "When you endure suffering, you use up your appointed share of suffering. Once your suffering and bad karma are gone, a new world will open up for you." Beethoven reached the peak of his career after he had gone deaf. Helen Keller was able to speak, read, write, and fight for the rights of the blind through her speeches and writings. Even though she was born deaf, mute, and blind, she taught people to appreciate the significance of life more profoundly. As the Master said: "With faith, anyone can contribute to our society. Even though the body is handicapped, the heart shouldn't be."

three

PHILOSOPHICAL CHALLENGES

18 } *A new philosophy of nursing education*

CHALLENGE: How does one teach kindness and compassion?

"Birth, aging, and sickness are nurtured by the dew and
the sunlight. Gentle compassion is able to ease the pain."
TZU CHI JUNIOR COLLEGE OF NURSING ANTHEM, BY KAO HSIN-CHIANG

Background

Not long after the Tzu Chi General Hospital opened in Hualien,
Master Cheng Yen decided to train a group of compassionate doctors and nurses, because the hospital was located in a remote area
and it was not easy to hire medical professionals to work there.
The Tzu Chi Junior College of Nursing was founded in 1989 and
was the first step toward the Tzu Chi mission of education.

Challenge

Although it was the Master's first attempt at setting up a school,
she already had ideals and expectations for the nursing college.
She wanted the students to receive a good academic education,
but also a warm "family education," which would teach them how
to get along with and respect other people. In addition to hiring
instructors to teach the classes, Master Cheng Yen established
the Yi Te Mother/Father Association, in which three commissioners are assigned to look after each group of nine students.

These "mothers" and "fathers" apply the Buddha's compassion for all people and regard the students as their own daughters. The students can talk to them about problems that they feel unable to discuss with their instructors.

Some years ago I acted as a "father" to a group of students, and I recently met up with some of them. They are working in different places. As we chatted, they told me they are often praised for their good attitude toward work. I asked them if that makes them proud. My "daughters" all replied humbly, "No, it reminds us to show more respect to other people." They continued: "Sometimes patients even ask us where we received our degrees, and we say, 'Tzu Chi Junior College of Nursing,' and they say, 'Tzu Chi? No wonder!'" Listening to them talk, I could sense and share in their joy.

The nursing college (now part of the Tzu Chi College of Technology) also places much emphasis on the humanities, so the school teaches classes on tea ceremony, flower arrangement, Zen meditation, music, and sign language. The Master firmly believes that education is not just about passing down professional skills or knowledge; above all, it must nurture students' minds. As nurses, they will be saving people's lives, so they should nurture their humanitarianism and their spirit of kindness, compassion, joy, and unselfish giving. The Master tells the students repeatedly that each one of them will become a white-robed Kuan Yin, the Bodhisattva of Compassion, whose job will be to take good care of their patients. She encourages every student with these expectations, and with help from the Yi Te Mother/Father Association and the humanities classes, the nursing college has not let her down.

To ensure equal access to the college, Taiwanese aboriginal girls are offered free tuition. The five-year aboriginal classes accept aboriginal girls who have graduated from junior high school. Although not many girls applied at first, through referrals from local government offices and through word of mouth, the classes are filled to capacity. Many aboriginal girls in junior high schools in Hualien aim to enter the nursing college.

Effects and Reflections

Many people criticize Taiwan's educational system for being too focused on academics. Teachers burden their students with frequent examinations, and many make the students spend every second of their time studying, even late into the night. Although education is about teaching skills and knowledge, what is more important is developing students' personalities.

To ensure the college's students become professional nurses with the compassion of Kuan Yin Bodhisattva, the Master has hired many teachers and individuals who teach not only medical skills but set good examples for students to follow and let students learn to interact with each other in a family atmosphere. (The medical college, which was set up after the nursing college, uses this same educational system, including the "Tzu-cheng Fathers Association," an organization similar to the Yi Te Association.)

Johann Heinrich Pestalozzi, who is considered one of the greatest reformers in the history of teaching, said two hundred years ago that if public education were to be valuable to humanity, it had to adopt the merits of family instruction. The Swiss educator also stated that "the sole and everlasting foundation" of education is love for those we teach. This ideology is used in the Tzu Chi Junior College of Nursing and in extracurricular classes such as the Tzu Chi Collegiate Youth Association camps and Buddhist studies camps for children and teenagers.

Graduates from the nursing college work in many hospitals around Taiwan. They are like seeds of love spreading the compassion of Kuan Yin Bodhisattva to every corner of their hospitals.

19 } *The land around Liyu Lake*

CHALLENGE: When should one turn away from beauty?

"Human beings are nurtured by all kinds of things produced
and grown on the Earth, so we must care for our natural
resources with gratitude and allow the Earth to maintain
its beauty." MASTER CHENG YEN

Background

Master Cheng Yen wanted to set up an elementary school, a secondary school, and a university to extend the spirituality and
wisdom of Buddhism. In doing so, the Tzu Chi mission of education would be carried on generation after generation.

Because of the success of the Tzu Chi hospital, the Tzu Chi
Junior College of Nursing, and the Tzu Chi College of Medicine,
many Taiwanese have recognized the Master's sincerity and accomplishments. She often receives enthusiastic offers to help realize her
dreams. Such was the case when the Master announced her plan
to establish a university: a benefactor offered a fairly large piece
of land near picturesque Liyu Lake, just south of Hualien. Those
who saw the lot were very impressed by the beautiful scenery, and
they strongly recommended that the Master accept this offer.

With her disciples, the Master went to see this "dream land,"
a tract of virgin land with a lake that reflected the green forests

of the surrounding mountains. One would be most refreshed and joyful after taking a stroll there. "This place is truly astonishing," exclaimed the Master after she had walked around the lake. As her disciples were all voicing their agreement that the university had to be built on this piece of land, the Master unexpectedly stunned them by saying slowly, "Unfortunately, we cannot use it."

Challenge

The disciples were dumbfounded. The Master shook her head, explaining, "It's not that I don't like it—it's that I like it too much. It's because I like it so much that I don't want to occupy it and destroy it." The Master continued, "I constantly appeal to the public to protect our environment and to love our land. But if we used this place, we would have to cut down trees and dig up the earth, and the beautiful scenery around the lake would be destroyed."

One commissioner did not want to give up so easily and asked, "Master, you may turn down this offer to build a university here now, but won't you regret it later?" The Master replied firmly, "I have a responsibility to protect the environment . . . Pure love is giving, not occupying." Although the Master wanted to continue the mission of education, in her heart, environmental protection is as important as education because both of them are for the development and prosperity of future generations. As a result, she refused to sacrifice one for the other.

Effects and Reflections

The Master was willing to give up a very beautiful piece of land to uphold her idea of protecting the environment. Her decision to give up the land meant that future generations would be able to enjoy the beautiful sights. What an unselfish love that was! She also encourages the public to say no to disposable bowls and chopsticks (commonly used at food stalls and cafeterias in Taiwan). Instead, she urges Tzu Chi members to carry their own bowls, chopsticks, and drinking cups whenever they go out so that they produce less garbage. Tzu Chi volunteers carry out recycling initiatives in every community to reduce damage to the environment, and they pick garbage off the ground and sort it into recyclable and nonrecyclable materials because they love the world we live in and desire to leave a Pure Land for our future generations.

After the Master gave up the land around Liyu Lake, it was very hard for Tzu Chi to find a new piece of land. (Eventually, property was secured and the school was built.) However, the Master has never regretted her decision: as she constantly informs every Tzu Chi member, "We don't just talk about Tzu Chi's ideology—we demonstrate it with our actions." The foundation always carries out environmental impact surveys on its sites and insists on never building on mountainous slopes.

Like the Master, we would do well to stick to our principles. Because of her love for nature and the environment, the Master didn't want to occupy the land and destroy it. She treats the environment with respect, just as she does human beings. When we love someone, we try to understand his or her needs and give appropriate care and assistance, so he or she can grow and become strong. We hope everyone can have this pure, unselfish love for those they care about, for the Earth, and for everything on this planet. In this way, we can maintain harmony between people, and between people and nature.

20 } *Interpreting unexpected events*

CHALLENGE: What is the nature of miracles,
omens, and supernatural powers?

"When our spirit is collected and everything goes as we
wish, that is 'supernatural power.' Real Buddhism does not
strive after extra senses or supernatural power. Our undefiled
hearts are the places to seek buddhas." MASTER CHENG YEN

Background

In March 1986, renovations at the Abode of Still Thoughts were
almost complete. The rooms had been updated and a new two-
story dormitory for volunteers had been added to the right of the
main hall. There is still no shining gold temple. The simple, quiet,
gray-colored Abode continues to offer visitors a sense of ordinari-
ness, harmony, and friendliness. Tzu Chi members from around
the world came to visit their "spiritual home," which had constantly appeared in their dreams.

One drizzly day, as everyone got off the bus and walked
toward the main sanctuary, the rain suddenly stopped. Looking
up at the sky, some visitors noticed two clouds moving toward
each other and forming the shape of a lotus flower right above the
Abode. When the sun shone from behind the clouds, it looked as
though the divine light of good fortune was radiating from the

lotus flower. Many people shouted with joy when they witnessed this "miracle," and some snapped pictures of it on the spot.

Challenge

Was this shining lotus flower in the sky a miracle? The crowds were still talking excitedly about it as they entered the main sanctuary of the Abode. Some said that with the renovations almost finished, a lotus flower in the sky had to be a good omen. Some said that if they published their photos, more people would join Tzu Chi, providing much-needed volunteers for the hospital.

As she listened to the crowd talk about the miracle, the Master simply smiled. However, when she heard someone suggest distributing the photo to the public, she said calmly, "What you saw was only a coincidence, so there is no need to have the photos developed, nor should you spread reprints to other people." She stopped for a moment and continued with much emphasis, "I hope people join Tzu Chi because of my convictions, not because of my 'supernatural power.'" No "miracle photos" have been published by Tzu Chi.

Effects and Reflections

Some religions regard miracles as being the most effective tool with which to attract believers: we often hear of sects that use so-called "miracle photographs" or "supernatural powers" to entice large groups of believers. Because of this, many people equate religion with superstition.

In 1999, China's Central TV station sent a crew to Taiwan to film Tzu Chi activities. The producer of the program was at first rather skeptical about what Tzu Chi did, because he believed most Buddhists were superstitious. But after he came to Taiwan and heard the Master say, "It is better to be atheist than superstitious," his attitude changed completely. The Master is absolutely opposed to anyone seeking refuge in Buddhism or joining Tzu Chi because of his or her own superstitions. The Master never talks about supernatural power, and she never disguises the fact that she is often physically weak.

I remember one day a relative of a Tzu Chi member suffered from a nervous breakdown. This member hoped the Master could bless and cure his relative by touching his head. The Master shook her head, "If my touch could alleviate his illness, then I wouldn't have needed to build a hospital. I can't help you, so you should take him to see a psychiatrist at the Tzu Chi Hospital."

Similarly, feng shui (Chinese geomancy—literally "wind and water") is still very popular among the general public in Taiwan, but the Master's explanation is: "Any place with wind [good ventilation] and water is a place with good feng shui." Likewise, when people often ask the Master to pick a lucky date on which to start a construction project, the Master always replies, "A 'good date' in Taiwan may not be a 'good date' in the United States. Thus, it is impossible to pick a date that everyone likes. For me, a 'good date' is when the workers, the construction materials, and all related aspects are ready."

As the Master once said, "supernatural power" just means that when everyone works together with one spirit, they will be successful in everything they do. We often see the Master display her "supernatural powers" of extraordinary concentration and willpower. Everything she thinks about, everything she does is for this human world. She becomes sick, takes medicine and, like everyone else, feels happiness, grief, and sadness. The difference is that she is able to transform these negative emotions, and also change the mindset and the actions of all Tzu Chi members, so that she can face her problems positively and try to solve them.

Master Cheng Yen is generous and frank enough to let us see her true human self. Each "Tzu Chi miracle" is created every day under her guidance, but she attributes each one of them to the hard work of every Tzu Chi member and also to everyone who contributes silently. She constantly teaches us that we are all equal to the Buddha in terms of our intrinsic buddha-nature, that we should nurture our wisdom and correct beliefs and not become superstitious. "We should depend on ourselves, not the gods," she says. With her wisdom, she teaches people that with the right beliefs, they can bring tranquillity to their bodies and minds and march positively toward a life of faith.

21 } *Maintaining political independence*

CHALLENGE: How can politics and religion co-exist?

"Tzu Chi cares about society but is not involved in politics."
MASTER CHENG YEN

Background

A Tzu Chi commissioner in Yungho, Taipei County, was thinking of running for election, so she went to see the Master. The Master asked her, "Why do you want to enter politics?"

The commissioner replied, "Because I want to understand what the public thinks and I want to serve society."

The Master countered, "Tzu Chi members are in constant contact with the public, so we always understand what people are thinking. And we are helping society, aren't we?"

This advice changed the woman's mind. She is still a Tzu Chi commissioner, is in constant contact with the public, and gives service to society every day, and she is much more joyful now.

Challenge

History reminds us that when politics and religion mix, more often than not tragedy will occur. The Master understands that if these two forces become intertwined, both sides will become distorted and misrepresented. The foundation thus established a rule that prohibits its members from being involved in politics.

As Tzu Chi's membership increases, its influence also rises and it becomes difficult to maintain a safe distance from politics. In the past, the ruling Nationalist Party of Taiwan invited Master Cheng Yen or her disciples to become delegates in the legislature, but the Master always turned down the offer and refuses to publicly support individual candidates.

Despite the fact that political participation provides access to quick, practical, and useful political resources, which could help to advance Tzu Chi's objectives, the Master still firmly refuses to join. She hopes all Tzu Chi members contribute to society with pure minds, not with any desire for power. She also knows that if Tzu Chi commissioners or nuns work hard on charitable activities but later decide to participate in politics, their original good intentions may be questioned. The Master doesn't want any Tzu Chi member to be open to question.

Effects and Reflections

Master Cheng Yen often warns Tzu Chi members, "We should be concerned about politics and society, but not politically involved." Whenever a political issue arises, Tzu Chi always maintains a peaceful and nonconfrontational attitude and solves the problem through peaceful dialogue. She also says frequently, "Voting is the responsibility of every citizen; choosing the right person to govern is the duty of every citizen." However, she also tells us not to be involved in politics, not to run for election or help anyone else run for election. She wants every Tzu Chi member to maintain a pure heart when making contributions, to avoid the temptation of power as well as the possibility of being questioned by society.

It has become part of Tzu Chi culture that no members talk about politics or try to persuade anyone one way or the other. Anyone breaching this regulation is admonished by other Tzu

Chi members. In fact, Lin Ming-ying, candidate Lin Yang-kang's daughter and a Tzu Chi commissioner, wanted to help her father in the 1996 presidential election, so she returned her commissioner's ID card to the Master. Many people had heard of this rule, but they had never realized the Master was so strict in enforcing it. Thus, all Tzu Chi members regard each other as equal, even if they hold different political views. As the Master teaches, "Let politics be politics, religion be religion." It is the most basic symbol of a democratic society.

22 } *Defusing misunderstandings with other groups*

CHALLENGE: How can one learn from criticism?

"The best response to others' suspicions is to remain undisturbed by negative emotions and resolutely do the right things." MASTER CHENG YEN

Background
A Buddhist monk once phoned the Master and reproved her for not allowing Tzu Chi disciples to receive alms, because the Master's self-reliance had placed other Buddhist monks and nuns in a very awkward situation. The Master listened quietly to the complaint and didn't argue. When they hung up, the Master was worried that this monk might still be very angry, so she phoned him back to apologize. The Master first humbly accepted the criticism and then explained her position. Forgiveness, tolerance, and humility are her ways of dealing with others' suspicions. She tries to take others' viewpoints into consideration, not just her own. The next day the Master unexpectedly ran into similar censure, but this time in front of her own disciples. She still didn't argue, she just kept apologizing.

Challenge
The Master reminds her followers that misunderstandings among people are unavoidable and it hurts to be criticized. "Having

realized this, we should not criticize other people," she proclaims. She adds that the Buddha stipulated that monks and nuns could receive offerings from the public, and she has never said that they shouldn't do so. She, personally, has made a different choice: she accepts only spiritual offerings, and she receives many offerings from Tzu Chi members! She says, "We nuns at Tzu Chi receive offerings from the public's actions [doing good deeds] and identification [identifying with the Tzu Chi ideals and concepts]."

As Tzu Chi grows, there is skepticism about its motivations and methods, both from Buddhists and from other groups. Many claim that when devoted Buddhists choose to shave their heads and become monks or nuns, they try to leave this lowly world behind, carry out their spiritual cultivation, and attempt to attain enlightenment for themselves by diligently cultivating their buddha-nature before trying to help others attain enlightenment. When the Tzu Chi Foundation began to carry out charity work and build hospitals and schools in this spirit, some people misunderstood the Master's desire to "look for Buddha's teachings in this world." There are always Tzu Chi members who feel hurt by this criticism and want to debate it; however, the Master keeps telling them not to feel hurt so easily and not to create more friction.

Effects and Reflections

We may remain silent when we hear different viewpoints, but why don't we respond to criticisms that are wrong? The Master explained that we should treat disputes as education, praise as warnings, dislike as reflection, and mistakes as experiences. Any criticism should be considered a valuable reminder. She said that when there is wrong, it can be made right, and when there is evil, it can be made good. If we can face a dispute with an understanding attitude, there won't be any dispute. "Furthermore, Tzu Chi has so many things to do, so long as we behave honorably, we don't need to explain any of our deeds," she added.

Although rational debate can help to clarify the truth, the Master always reflects on herself first and then uses her endeavors and reality itself to enlighten others on the matter. This unites all Tzu Chi members in an unspoken consensus: there are so many things to do that there is no time to defend ourselves, because we want to spend most of our time doing other things. We accept true criticisms humbly and take untrue ones as education. As years go by, there is less and less criticism and far more understanding than misunderstanding.

The Master's instruction to all Tzu Chi members on how to face criticism is an excellent reinforcement of cognitive behavioral psychology, which states that every negative emotion can influence and imprison us; it can also influence our behavior in a negative way. Listening to criticism without reacting to it ensures we may do things with peace of mind and not behave irrationally. We will then be able to express Tzu Chi's ideals little by little.

23 } *Showing respect for Buddhism*

CHALLENGE: How does one guide
changes in behavior?

"When you behave with decorum,
your mind can be righteous."
MASTER CHENG YEN

Background

People think of Tzu Chi members as being kind and gentle people
who always face the public cheerfully. But the public may not
know that in addition to participating actively in social services,
Master Cheng Yen is also very strict, both with herself and with
all Tzu Chi members, in following Buddhist etiquette.

However, as the *Earth Treasury Sutra* points out, all living
beings have their deep-rooted habits, and it is not easy to change
and follow strict regulations. Furthermore, many people mis-
takenly think that the Buddha's teachings only train their mind,
not their behavior. Nevertheless, the Master has her own way of
making Tzu Chi members follow the rules.

Challenge

Sister Lin Yueh-yun is a very industrious commissioner who is
good at raising funds, and the other Tzu Chi members respect her

very highly. However, the Master once taught her a lesson during a seven-day Zen meditation camp.

On the first day, the Master as usual taught everyone how to wear the *haiching*, a light, black robe that lay Buddhists often wear during ceremonies, and she asked Lin and another senior member to demonstrate for the others the proper way to put it on. Lin saw the assignment as a piece of cake since she had gone to many Buddhist temples and received the Bodhisattva Precepts, a special certificate that only senior Buddhists are entitled to receive.

The Master first showed the audience how to do it, and then she asked Lin and the other senior member to do it again. The other woman was worried that she was very old and wouldn't do it well enough. She was mindful in putting on the *haiching*, and so she did it very well. However, experienced, confident Sister Lin kept making mistakes. The Master then said to her, "Look at you, you can't even put on the robe properly! Even this senior sister is better than you!" The audience burst into laughter, and Lin, who had been outstanding in many fields, experienced her first setback.

On the second day, the Master again taught everyone how to put on the *haiching*. Lin thought, "Again? She won't pick me this time, will she?" Unexpectedly, the Master called her up again. Sister Lin hadn't practiced at all. Therefore, she still didn't know how to put on the robe and everyone laughed even louder this time.

At noon, Master Te Ju pulled Lin aside and said to her, "Let's practice together, because I know the Master's way of teaching: when she wants to train someone, she'll keep at it until that person becomes an expert."

Lin said, "I don't believe the Master will teach us to put on the robe again. She has been teaching us how to put on the *haiching* for two days, so what will she teach for the next five days?"

Lin adamantly refused to learn how to put on the robe, but Master Te Ju didn't want her to lose face again, so she begged her to study how. Lin finally gave in, and the two of them went to a remote corner and practiced in secret. Without a sound, Master Cheng Yen walked up from behind and startled both of them. Before they pulled themselves together, the Master said, "Wouldn't you have been better off if you had learned how to do it more mindfully earlier?"

On the third day, the Master again taught everyone how to dress. Lin thought, "Master Te Ju was quite right; she knew the Master would teach us how to dress again. Now I'm fully prepared, so let's see how the Master will test me." And as usual, she was asked to step forward. Lin stood up confidently, but the Master said, "Today we won't learn how to put on the *haiching*; we will learn to put on the *manyi*." This dark brown robe is worn over the *haiching*, and only those who have received the basic Five Precepts may wear it.

Lin was much worse off this time, and everyone guffawed; even the Master was laughing. The Master asked someone to bring over a mirror, and when Lin saw herself in the mirror, she was ashamed. "I wanted to dig a hole in the floor and hide," recalled Lin with embarrassment.

The Master said to Lin, "I see you as a piece of cypress wood that won't break when I hit you; if you were only a piece of rotten wood, you would break apart."

Lin admired the Master's courage in dealing with her. Lin was quite skillful at raising money, and when she joined Tzu Chi, a large number of her friends had joined with her. If the Master had ridiculed Lin too hard, she wouldn't have been the only one to leave the foundation. Lin said that if the Master's way of teaching had not been quite so straightforward, she would not have been able to learn anything. Indeed, the Master might even have destroyed her will to improve herself.

Effects and Reflections

Confucius once said that we should teach according to the intellectual faculty of our students, by understanding what sort of people the students are and finding the right path to teach them. The Master actually wanted to eliminate Lin's arrogance so Lin could understand that she could learn new things only with a humble mind.

The Master's way of teaching is divided into three steps: praise, criticism, and then self-examination by the disciples themselves. She often says that when you teach someone, you must teach at the right time. If you praise someone at the wrong time, your praise will hurt that person. Similarly, when you criticize someone at the wrong time, your criticism will hurt that person. I think the Master can determine the proper time through her penetrating judgment of each person's intellectual qualities.

When we teach people, we have to set a good example for them to follow. If we can't do so, then everything we do will be in vain. Thus, the Master always lives up to the rules she wants her disciples to follow.

Take the morning prayers as an example. The disciples are quite concerned for the Master's frail health, so they ask her not to lead the daily morning service, but the Master always insists on attending the service from beginning to end. The Master participates every day whenever seven-day Buddhist meditation camps are held.

She is quite strict with the ways in which she, and every Tzu Chi member, eats, dresses, sits, and sleeps. While eating, our hands must be poised like "a dragon's mouth holding a pearl and a phoenix drinking water." We must hold the rice bowl in the left hand with the thumb pressing lightly on the rim and the other four fingers supporting the bowl at its base. In this way, the hand looks like the mouth of a dragon holding the "pearl" of the rice bowl. "A phoenix drinking water" means that we should move the chopsticks elegantly and swiftly, like a phoenix drinking water. In this way we show the dignity of Buddhist practitioners.

The Master also asks for dignity in our dress. She often says, "When you behave with decorum, then your mind can be righteous." At every Tzu Chi gathering, female commissioners must fold their hair up in a bun, a style called the "Tzu Chi hairdo." They put on a navy-blue Chinese *chipao*, "the Dress of Gentleness and Tolerance," or a blue shirt and white pants, which is called "the Blue Sky and White Cloud Outfit." The men also wear a blue shirt and white pants.

Our home should be tidy and clean, not disorganized or messy. We must not throw things around. When we walk, we should walk gently. Furthermore, the Master says that even when we have a good heart, if we have a bad temper and use foul language, we are not a decent person. So we have to be careful when we interact with other people, and our actions must be in accord with our mind. We should not be distracted while we act.

According to Chu Hsi, a great thinker in the Sung Dynasty (960–1279) in ancient China who unified philosophical thoughts from the past with those from his own time, a person's appearance is the first step toward learning the importance of self-respect. For instance, he stressed the importance of how one dresses. If a person is rather loose with his clothes and hair, then he or she is not dignified and will often be looked down upon. In Chu Hsi's view, everyone should keep his or her body straight, take care of his or her clothes, hat, socks, and shoes, and keep them all clean. Tzu Chi maintains this precept as a priority in personal training; it is a reminder that the Buddha's teachings train not only the mind, but also one's behavior.

24 } *Observing from all angles*

CHALLENGE: How does one become wise?

"Wisdom is generated from our interactions with
other people and events. If you pay attention to every
matter in life, your wisdom will naturally grow."
MASTER CHENG YEN

Background

How can a nun who has received little formal education and who
has never set foot on foreign soil have the wisdom and vision to
lead Tzu Chi members in an ever-growing foundation that han-
dles multiple missions at the same time? To better understand
how the Master does this, Kao Hsin-chiang, the former president
of *China Times Express*, once asked the Master, "How do you per-
ceive the world?"

The Master replied, "Most people put a flower on a piece of
white paper to look at it, but the true observer places it on a piece
of glass."

To look at a flower on a piece of white paper is like looking at
a painting: the flower is an isolated, lifeless subject. You don't see
the environment around it or the causes that created the flower.
But if you place the flower on a piece of transparent glass, you can
see the relationship between the flower, its natural background,
and the universe. Every spot you look at illuminates the causes,

the conditions, and the joy of life. Therefore, the flower won't be just one single flower.

Challenge

Clearly, advanced education and abundant travel experiences do not necessarily lead to foresight and good judgment. So, how can one absorb knowledge and enhance wisdom?

Besides reading books and news reports from many sources to gain a thorough understanding of major events around the world, the Master also reads the "wonderful human scripture." Because she comes into contact with Tzu Chi members from all walks of life every day, she is able to absorb new knowledge, ideas, ways of thinking, and valuable suggestions. The Master also receives many visitors from all over the world, including scholars, businesspeople, politicians, religious leaders, and the elite from every sector of society. As she once said, "Every day is a new page in life."

Someone asked the Master why, even though some people read books and deal with all sorts of people every day, their minds are still full of obstacles and delusion. The Master answered that to truly listen to a person's message we must empty our minds first and listen without preconceived notions. We must also concentrate fully on what is happening at every moment, because the future is delusion and the past is distraction. Our wisdom will improve only when we are fully aware of the moment. This is how the Master perceives the world, so she is able to see more widely, clearly, and completely.

Effects and Reflections

What is wisdom? Will Durant, an American philosopher who wrote many books in his life and translated profound classics into fascinating philosophical works, once gave a wise answer to this question: "Wisdom is observing from all perspectives." Because the Master is an active listener, feels grateful all the time, and has tolerance for all kinds of people, she is able to exercise Great Love. The source of the Master's wisdom and strength lies in her observations from all angles and her attentive listening. Tzu Chi members are, in effect, the Master's hands and eyes.

This is how Tzu Chi is organized. The Master is the chair of the board of directors for all Tzu Chi establishments—local, regional, and international. Under the Master, there is a department of religious practice; under this department, there are commissioners, who are specially appointed by the Master. The commissioners will look after all Tzu Chi establishments. One commissioner chairs each regional and international Tzu Chi chapter, the Tzu Chi hospital, and the Tzu Chi college, as well as the television station established by Tzu Chi.

Tzu Chi members report on the activities of the local chapters, and they also come to the Master with problems and questions pertinent to local business and relief programs. She receives oral reports, written documents, photographs, and videotapes. She sees all the causes and effects behind the events and finds out the true reasons why they happened. This way she experiences all the suffering and warmth in life by means of the materials provided by her disciples.

In our own lives, we can become wise by watching our own blind spots, listening with gratitude, truly observing from all perspectives, and pushing our own boundaries of time, place, and ego.

four

EXPANSION
AND RENEWAL

25 } *The Master's disciples*

CHALLENGE: Why are there so few nuns?

"If people can apply otherworldly spirit to
worldly affairs, they can all become bodhisattvas."
MASTER CHENG YEN

Background

In Buddhism, there are few requirements for people who wish
to become monks or nuns, as long as they are willing to dedicate themselves to Buddhism and are willing to have their heads
shaved. As a Buddhist nun, Master Cheng Yen can only consecrate her female followers. (Buddhist monks can consecrate both
male and female followers.) However, the Master is always very
serious when it comes to accepting laywomen as nuns. If women
insist on becoming nuns without permission from their families,
they will simply create conflicts.

Challenge

In theory, Buddhism will spread if more people become nuns and
monks. When more nuns join Tzu Chi, there will be more of
them to disseminate the Buddha's message and to carry out the
growing number of Tzu Chi missions.

For a long time, many women from every sector of society have
hoped to become nuns under the Master's tutelage. Some of them

hold doctorates or medical degrees or are experts in special fields. However, the Master never accepts them simply because of their background; instead she is very strict about who she accepts since becoming a monk or a nun is a lifetime matter. Just as the decision to marry must not be made based upon passion or impulse, neither should the decision to become a nun. In reality, becoming a nun is much harder than getting married, and a nun often shoulders more responsibility educating people and relieving suffering. If the nuns can't handle the pressure, they will suffer miserably.

The Master insists on two conditions when women want to become nuns. First, those with professional expertise must consider applying their skills in the job market and must not enter religious life without giving it thorough consideration. Second, those with husbands or children must discuss the decision with their families first and receive their permission. Young, single women must receive their parent's agreement in writing, in addition to thoroughly considering their choice of leaving home. (This is to remind these young people that they must think about their duties to their parents, so there will be fewer family confrontations.) Then they may join the order.

There is a saying: "It is easy to become a monk or a nun, but difficult to carry out spiritual cultivation. It is easy to shave off one's hair, but difficult to devote one's mind to Buddhism." For this reason, prospective nuns must be postulants for two years before they are officially consecrated as nuns. What the Master stresses the most is not the nuns' superficial appearance, but their inner cultivation and the practice of the Buddha's teachings. In the early days, the Master's disciples had to study and memorize the *Analects of Confucius*.

After the postulants complete their training and become nuns, they do not just recite Buddhist scriptures. They also plant crops or do other work, and they must practice their spiritual cultivation along with their assigned work. The Master hopes her postulants will comprehend that to become a nun is to devote all one's efforts to society without anything holding them back.

Effects and Reflections

The Master demands more from her nuns than from her lay followers. Because the Master is quite disciplined and careful when it comes to the decision to shave a female follower's head and consecrate her as a nun, only a few disciples out of her millions of followers can actually become nuns. Although the number of nuns is so small, there are many lay followers.

Tzu Chi members come from all walks of life. They include homemakers, businesspeople, workers, scholars, farmers, laborers, doctors, and lawyers. Many of them devote themselves to public welfare work in all corners of our society. The Master is grateful to them, but she also reminds them constantly to look after their own families as well as the Tzu Chi missions. They can't ignore their own family members or overlook their duties at home.

Anyone, Buddhist or not, can join Tzu Chi as long as they have love to give and like to help the needy. The Master respects all religions, and she often tells her lay followers that though they are not nuns, they can still do work with a worldly mind, apply the Buddhist teachings in their workplaces, and contribute greatly to society.

For those who are interested in studying the Buddha's teachings, the Master reminds them to practice what they have learned in their daily lives. The Master says, "We must learn the Buddha's confidence, resolution, and courage, and also his spirit of self-sacrifice for the greater good." Therefore, she objects to superstition, credulity, and any conduct aimed at rejecting other religions.

26 } *Building an organizational infrastructure*

CHALLENGE: How does one nurture humanitarians?

"Structure Tzu Chi according to the precepts and
manage it with love." MASTER CHENG YEN

Background

When Master Cheng Yen and her disciples established the Buddhist Compassion Relief Tzu Chi Foundation, it was only a small
organization. A year later, in 1967, there were about three hundred members. Clearly the Master could not oversee all of them,
and she trained ten commissioners to help organize and carry
out Tzu Chi missions. In just a few decades, Tzu Chi has grown
tremendously in size and has made great leaps in the number of
people served. For instance, during the period of 1992–2006, the
Tzu Chi Vancouver chapter has raised over US$17.5 million and
served 750,000 clients. The number of volunteers who have participated in Tzu Chi Vancouver has climbed to 220,000. At any
time, there are about 3,000 volunteers serving in Greater Vancouver every month.

Master Cheng Yen, then, is the spiritual pillar of the foundation, and the commissioners and members are her faithful
followers who put her teachings into practice. Their words and
conduct directly represent the characteristics of the Tzu Chi spirit,
and so it is important that everyone follow the same vision. In a

rapidly growing organization, how does one ensure consistency of vision and effective communication?

Challenge

In the early days, to become a commissioner one had to earnestly and sincerely want to participate, identify with the Master's concepts, and be sponsored by a senior commissioner. After brief training and personal selection by the Master, one was eligible to become a commissioner.

As the number of commissioners grows, Master Cheng Yen is no longer able to personally train and select competent commissioners who possess both the Four Immeasurables (kindness, compassion, joy, and unselfish giving) and the Four Principles (sincerity, integrity, trust, and honesty). Hence she set up the code of conduct—the Ten Tzu Chi Precepts—which everyone involved with Tzu Chi must follow.

1. Do not kill.

2. Do not steal.

3. Do not fornicate.

4. Do not lie.

5. Do not drink alcohol.

6. Do not smoke, use drugs, or chew betel nuts.

7. Do not gamble or speculate on the stock market.

8. Do not lose your temper; be humble and loving.

9. Obey the law; follow traffic rules; do not participate in politics or demonstrations.

10. Respect your parents and be moderate in speech and attitude.

The first five precepts are the Five Precepts of Buddhism, and the last five were dictated by the Master. She also wants everyone to actively practice the Tzu Chi spirit in their daily lives.

For an organization to become stable in the long term, the organizational structure plays an important role. To become a commissioner today, one must undergo two years of training. In the first year, potential commissioners attend a variety of classes so that they may profoundly understand the Tzu Chi spirit. Once they have completed the classes, they become commissioner trainees who accompany official commissioners and carry out Tzu Chi tasks for a full year. Only then can they officially become commissioners.

Collecting donations is one of the main tasks of the commissioners. The Master's main intention is not for them to collect money, but to collect the love hidden in people's hearts. By collecting donations, the commissioners get to know members and help them resolve their problems. Through understanding and helping others, the commissioners also have the chance to look at their own lives and cultivate their spirituality as well as working with others to carry out the Tzu Chi missions. Through all this, they learn the true meaning of life.

Effects and Reflections
"Structure Tzu Chi according to the precepts and manage it with love" reflects the full spiritual meaning of the commissioners' training courses. As the number of members increases, using the precepts to standardize the conduct of Tzu Chi people is the most sensible and efficient management method. Precepts such as "Do not participate in politics or demonstrations" and "Do not drink alcohol" might be too strict for some people, but Tzu Chi

is a Buddhist charity organization and the commissioners represent Tzu Chi. Hence the precepts for the commissioners are of a higher standard than those for people from the general public. Members subconsciously encourage and learn from each other under the effect of the precepts, ensuring not only the conscientious and dignified behavior of Tzu Chi commissioners, but also their mutual commitment to the organization and its teachings.

Tzu Chi is entirely self-managed by the initiative and interaction of the members. What Master Cheng Yen does is draw out everyone's faith in Tzu Chi and purify their attitudes toward life, and then allow them to voluntarily take part in Tzu Chi activities and manage themselves.

Harvard University Professor Frederick Schauer (an expert on the First Amendment of the Constitution of the United States) has stated: "Neither rules nor codes are self-enforcing, and a rule or code has force only for an agent who accepts or internalizes that rule or code. The task, then, is to think of incentives or other factors which would lead an agent to accept some rule or code." Tzu Chi commissioners accept the precepts because of the good examples set by Master Cheng Yen and other senior commissioners, and also because they identify with Tzu Chi's convictions and methods. They participate with enthusiasm, and they obviously have much stronger self-motivation and self-discipline than most people. Because members of Tzu Chi willingly accept and follow the precepts, they act sincerely and with unfailing goodwill.

27 } *Creating a shared vision*

CHALLENGE: How does one build a
team from a group of individuals?

"Tzu Chi missions are accomplished by
teamwork, not by individual action.
Good deeds must be based on compassion
and wisdom so that they will endure."
MASTER CHENG YEN

Background
A Tzu Chi volunteer kindly took in a child who had just been
released from a reformatory. This child had grown up in a single-
parent family with a father who had a serious tendency toward
violence. In turn, the child had committed acts of violence.

Under the care and influence of the Tzu Chi member, the
child's behavior improved remarkably. When it came time to
consider a permanent home for the child, the judge asked the volunteer if she would like to continue looking after the child and, if
possible, take in a few more children with similar backgrounds.

The volunteer and the child had grown to love each other and
wanted to continue living together. However, the child's father
refused to be separated from his child, and he threatened the
safety of the volunteer's family. Extremely worried, the volunteer
asked Master Cheng Yen for advice.

Challenge

After listening to the story, the Master asked the Tzu Chi volunteer a few questions:

"Does your husband approve of and agree to your taking care of the child?"

"He doesn't support my actions," the sister replied.

"What was the father's attitude when you took in the child?"

"He was very angry," answered the sister. "I heard that he's trying to find my home, and he's very threatening."

"Think about it," the Master solemnly told her. "Two fathers disagree with your keeping this child. Even if you do keep him, you cannot guarantee your future safety. You have created problems for two families. Is this appropriate?"

When the woman heard the Master's comment, she was speechless.

The Master continued, "Does looking after the child take up a lot of your time?"

"Certainly, I spend half of my time looking after him."

"That's right, you lose the time to do the things you want to do or need to do while looking after this child. Taking care of this boy is a good thing, but it results in problems for two families. More importantly, the father's wish to be reunited with his son is natural. Your good intentions have not only induced his anger but may also have endangered you and your family. What if something goes wrong? Isn't there any other way?"

The volunteer suddenly understood the Master's principle "Never harm one person for the sake of saving another." She quickly contacted family counselors, hoping that a team of professionals could help the boy and his father and save their family. With their combined experience, they could handle this case much better than she could alone.

Effects and Reflections

Master Cheng Yen often says, "Good deeds must be based on compassion and wisdom so that they will endure." All charity activities are cautiously evaluated, collectively discussed, and analyzed by experts before they are carried out. Master Cheng Yen hopes that all Tzu Chi missions will be accomplished through teamwork, not just by individuals. For example, relief funds must be distributed only under the name of Tzu Chi, rather than of any individual, so that recipients do not put Tzu Chi volunteers in an awkward position by asking them privately for assistance. Distributing relief funds through Tzu Chi is fairer and more reasonable, and it benefits everyone.

Similarly, the Master always responds to a compliment by saying, "This is not my personal achievement—it's the achievement of all Tzu Chi people." Tzu Chi is an organization of team players, and everyone has his or her work to do. It's not an individual effort: because everyone aspires to the convictions of Tzu Chi, every member shares in the achievements of the foundation.

As management expert Peter M. Senge wrote in the preface to the Chinese edition of his book *The Fifth Discipline*, "[Teamwork] is a path based on reflection on our deepest aspirations . . . It is a path based on our innate capacity for generative conversation, for being more intelligent together than we can ever be separately. It is a path based on the primacy of the whole rather than the primacy of the part . . ." Doing good deeds requires the support of shared vision, which encourages everyone to do his or her best and learn from and cooperate with each other as part of a team. In this manner, all difficulties and problems are readily solved and the rewards are widely spread. In fact, says Senge, when a group of people truly works together with a shared vision, it can accomplish things that previously seemed impossible.

28 } *Designing the Still Thoughts Hall*

CHALLENGE: How does one create a
modest yet world-class facility?

"Still Thoughts Hall—a place that presents the
Tzu Chi spirit and represents a wordless sermon."
MASTER CHENG YEN

Background

With the increase in membership and larger, more complex activities, Tzu Chi urgently needed a large activity center. In 1988,
Master Cheng Yen resolved to build a grand, multifunctional
Buddhist hall, the Still Thoughts Hall. However, many people
questioned this decision when it was announced. They respected
and admired the Master's simple, thrifty life and the fact that
all funds raised were used for charity work. The Abode of Still
Thoughts, where the Master lived, was not an eye-catching place,
and its furnishings were quite simple and plain. The doubters
worried about committing a large amount of money to build the
Still Thoughts Hall, a place they were concerned would be no different from a garish temple.

Challenge

The Master assured her disciples that building the Still Thoughts
Hall would be in accordance with the teaching of her mentor,

Dharma Master Yin Shun. In her mind, the hall had to display the Tzu Chi spirit and be a place for wordless sermons on the Buddha's teachings. Its plans were different from those of usual temples in that it was designed more like a huge activity center for artistic and cultural events.

Inside the Still Thoughts Hall is an international conference hall, which is equipped for simultaneous multilingual translation and is thus able to hold international Buddhist, academic, and medical conferences. Galleries house original religious art collections from all parts of the world and important documents and relics of Tzu Chi's progress. There is a memorial hall to commemorate inspirational people and events and a lecture hall for social, cultural, and philosophical lectures to promote Buddhism. Also, the main office of the Tzu Chi Foundation is located in the Still Thoughts Hall.

As the Master does not believe in the traditional Chinese concept of choosing a lucky day for an inauguration ceremony, each part of the building was used immediately once its construction was complete. (Still Thoughts Hall began operation in 1995, but construction is still going as of this writing.) Numerous religious, educational, and cultural activities of different sizes have been held in the hall, and the Global Tzu Chi Day is held there in May every year. Thousands of overseas members come back to take part in the festivities and share the knowledge they have learned in doing social services. The Still Thoughts Hall, because it can accommodate so many people, has become a focal point for Tzu Chi activities.

When drawing up the plans for the building, the Master paid close attention to durability, since she hopes the hall will be a spiritual citadel for generations of Buddhists and Tzu Chi people.

Rather than putting terracotta tiles on the roof, she insisted on using more expensive copper tiles. Because Hualien is a wet and windy place, terracotta tiles would have required frequent maintenance. Copper tiles will not break, though they will eventually oxidize to a green color that is still visually appealing. In the long term, copper tiles were more practical and economical than terracotta tiles.

Effects and Reflections

The Still Thoughts Hall has become the most important cultural hall in eastern Taiwan, and it will be for many years to come. The hall is not just a place for Buddhists to pay formal visits; it represents the spirit of Buddhism and is a spiritual fortress for history, education, art, and religion.

Through electronic broadcasts of the activities taking place in the hall, people around the world have a chance to understand that the culture of Buddhism can be rich and diverse. In addition, many visitors to the hall have been inspired to become Tzu Chi volunteers and to walk on the Path of the Bodhisattvas. As Sir Winston Churchill once said, human beings create the space they live in, and in turn the space determines their personalities. The Still Thoughts Hall is a place of wisdom and spirit and it nurtures these in those who visit.

29 } *The nature of money*

CHALLENGE: How can fundraising generate
compassion, kindness, and generosity of spirit?

"Joining Tzu Chi's charitable activities is not just the privilege
of rich people. Everyone has the right to participate. It's true
that we need donations to carry out our missions, but money
is not the final issue here, nor is the amount of money being
raised. What's important is to activate loving concern for
others in every heart. " MASTER CHENG YEN

Background

The site designated for the Tzu Chi College of Medicine was a
large piece of flat, green land with a few farmhouses scattered on
it. From my perspective as a businessman, I saw it as an opportunity for investment, since the college would not be able to
completely occupy this huge piece of land. Stores would certainly
be built around the college, so I thought, why doesn't Tzu Chi buy
all the surrounding land before the developers get to it first? I fig-
ured that Tzu Chi would eventually benefit enormously from the
increase in land values and would be able to use the extra money
to fund more good deeds.

At the time, more and more members were donating money
to Tzu Chi, but Master Cheng Yen only put all that income into

individual bank accounts for specific uses. These accounts generated interest, but the Master would not allow the money to be invested elsewhere. I couldn't see any profit accruing from these funds, whereas I knew that if the money were used to buy stocks or real estate, more revenue could be earned and Tzu Chi could amass a tremendous fortune.

I suggested to the Master that she purchase the land around the medical college campus or put some of the donations into other investment projects. However, the Master didn't seem to be convinced, nor did she show any interest in carrying on the conversation. Undeterred, I analyzed the benefits of investing the money: "With more money, Tzu Chi will be able to do more things."

The Master was very quiet for some time, and then she suddenly said firmly, "There is no need to talk about it anymore. You are not the only one who has made these suggestions, and I don't agree with them."

Challenge

The Master knows full well the benefits of investing the money, and she acknowledges that the foundation really needs a lot of funds to carry out its charitable deeds. However, soliciting donations is not Tzu Chi's objective, and the amount of money collected is not important. The critical issue is activating love and concern for others in every heart. She said, "I hope everyone can come and cultivate the field of blessings, and I also hope every person can continue to give. We are helping the needy, but at the same time we also want to educate the rich to share what they have with the less fortunate. It is very important for us to activate their love, to teach them how to do good deeds, and to nurture the seed of compassion in them."

I now understand that if the foundation invests the money it receives, it will be no different from any other business, which would seriously violate Tzu Chi's ideals.

Effects and Reflections

As time goes by, I admire the Master's wisdom more and more. If Master Cheng Yen had accepted my idea about investing the donations, Tzu Chi's fortune would have increased many times. But what about the trust, dignity, and noble ideals of its members? Would the foundation still have had contact with so many people? The answer is that Tzu Chi would have become a multinational enterprise instead.

Because the Master always wants to do more but doesn't want to invest any of the money, the foundation's income is never enough to cover expenses. Tzu Chi is always prepared to help the needy, and so the foundation continues to need the public to donate money, goods, and outpourings of love and goodwill. In this way, the Master hopes that the love in every heart can be stimulated and that everyone has a chance to do good for others in the world.

That Tzu Chi is continually in the red also helps to make sure there can be no wrongdoing. If there were ever any financial impropriety, donations from the public would stop coming. Therefore, this insistence on a constant lack of funds is like a fail-safe device that helps the organization avoid making mistakes and reminds every member to work hard for and cherish the foundation.

When I joined Tzu Chi in 1987, I heard the Master mention that she wanted to begin a second phase of expansion for the Tzu Chi General Hospital, build the Tzu Chi Junior College of Nursing, and start several other construction projects. I estimated that this would cost tens of billions of dollars, which would be a huge burden on the commissioners. How would they raise so much money? But the Master always said she had faith, and the commissioners didn't think this was a challenge. They saw it as a chance to use the tangible construction work to entice intangible love, and the visible contributions to create invisible blessings.

I have finally realized that the Master's ideals have nothing to do with how much money is available, but with purifying human hearts and building a Pure Land in this world. Then, the Tzu Chi spirit will expand ever outward without change.

30 } *Managing time and multiple projects*

CHALLENGE: How can one use time mindfully?

"Life is short, so we must hasten our steps and
not drag our feet while doing things. We must
pick up our back foot as soon as our front foot
firmly touches the ground. Let the events of
yesterday drop from your mind, and focus on
what you must do today." MASTER CHENG YEN

Background

If you ask anyone today what they lack the most, "time" is at the
top of the list. It is okay to have many things to do, but the main
problem is worrying about it, since we cannot concentrate on what
is happening in the moment when we are stressed about what has
happened or what might occur.

When we are young, we are concerned about our schoolwork
and friendships. When we grow older, we become concerned
about love and finding a job. When we reach middle age, we must
worry about our family's daily needs and education for our children. When we are old, we are concerned about our health and
all sorts of illnesses. No one can be free from them. Nevertheless,
precious treasures like time and life decrease bit by bit while we
are worrying.

Challenge

One day a businessman asked the Master: "I have appointments all day long and I have endless tasks to do every day. There are also many problems that are difficult to solve. I never seem to have enough time and I am always under pressure. The Tzu Chi missions are so enormous, and I have noticed that you have endless things to do. So how do you manage your schedule and emotions?"

The Master replied, "My heart is like a mirror when I have so many visitors to see and things to do. When a person comes, his or her problem appears in my mind, and when he or she leaves, the problem is removed from my mind. So I can see the next person or attend to the next matter."

When we are doing one thing, we tend to be thinking about something else. As more and more matters start to weigh on our minds, more and more worries also pile up. We begin to get distracted, and we certainly can't get things done. Lothar J. Seiwert, a time management expert, once said that the things we don't finish will finish us. Therefore, the Master admonishes us to pay attention to the matters we are working on at the moment, since she says that we can finish things only when we focus on them.

Effects and Reflections

Master Cheng Yen counts time by the second. The Master said, "People like to say they are passing time day by day, but I say we must do so second by second. When it comes to doing good deeds, every second counts." It is this philosophy that also helps her to overcome setbacks.

When she feels upset and wants to give up, an inner voice says to her, "No one is forcing you to do all this! Think back to the moment when you decided to follow this path." Then the Master recalls the pool of blood on the hospital floor and her resolve is strengthened. In other words, "We must seize the day and always bear in mind this moment of enthusiasm that we have now." If we can maintain forever the moment of inspiration and determination and make it the driving force that motivates us, we will not waste time.

31 } *Measuring success as an organization*

CHALLENGE: How does one remain
humble in the face of praise?

"Transform your love into action. Your highest
achievement comes from the happiness you sense
from helping other people with your love."
MASTER CHENG YEN

Background

As the Tzu Chi Foundation has grown and its reach widened,
Master Cheng Yen has received numerous commendations from
Taiwan and abroad. For instance, in 1976 the Taiwan provincial government awarded Tzu Chi first place of all the temples
on the island for its public welfare work. In 1986, the Master
was awarded the Hua Hsia First Class Medal, Taiwan's second-
highest civilian honor. She received several awards in 1989, including the prestigious Social Services and Sciences Award from the
Taiwanese American Foundation in the United States. In 1991,
she was awarded the Ramon Magsaysay Award (the "Asian Nobel
Prize") for Community Leadership, and two years later she was
nominated for the Nobel Peace Prize. All sorts of awards and
praise continue to pour in from around the world, but the Master
remains humble.

Challenge

Master Cheng Yen does not take sole credit for Tzu Chi's success; instead she reminds us that the foundation's achievements are the result of teamwork. After the Magsaysay Award from the Philippines was presented to a representative of the Taipei Economic and Cultural Office in the Philippines (Taiwan's quasi-embassy), who received the award on the Master's behalf, the Master wrote in her letter of appreciation: "Ancient Chinese sages used to say, 'Nothing under heaven can be completed by one person; everything is done by people working together.' The sages also said, 'Nothing under heaven is completed in just one period; all is done by one person after another and by one generation after another.' The accomplishments of the Tzu Chi Foundation during the past two decades have been created by many hard-working Buddhists, Tzu Chi commissioners, foundation members, and every kind and loving person."

The prize money was US$30,000. The Master gave half of it to the Philippine government to help refugees of volcano eruptions, and the other half was used for relief work in China.

In 1993, the Chinese University of Hong Kong decided to present an honorary doctoral degree in social science to the Master. The university requires that any recipient of the degree receive it in person. However, since the Master suffers from angina pectoris, she never leaves the country. Although the disciples hoped the Master would make an exception and travel to Hong Kong to receive this honor, she thanked the university for its kindness but noted that she would not be able to go in person due to her health. The Master didn't think much more about it, though her disciples were somewhat disappointed. So everyone was delighted when, unexpectedly, the university allowed the Master's disciples to receive the degree on her behalf.

On another occasion, a foundation established by pop star Michael Jackson planned to offer its first outstanding social service award to the Master. When I heard the news, I was more than excited. I knew that Jackson's name would surely attract attention to this award, which would be great publicity for Tzu Chi. I did all I could to persuade the Master: "Medical science is so advanced now that you can just carry your heart medicine with you. Medical professionals can also accompany you to the ceremony, so you won't be in any danger from flying for about ten hours."

The Master didn't say a word. Even worse, she gave me a stern glance. After the Master declined the award, it was presented instead to Elizabeth Taylor, who is known for her tireless efforts in support of the rights of AIDS patients. When I saw the award presentation on TV, I understood the Master's reasoning. It looked like an award ceremony for a superstar, filled with singing, dancing, and flashing lights. Although the award was set up with very good intentions, its style went completely against the Master's personality.

Effects and Reflections

Some people work hard for the sake of fame and fortune, but they often have nothing in the end. Even if they do achieve this goal, it is usually superficial and unreal. Wise people emphasize the process and the hard work, and fame comes to them in the long run. Not many people can look beyond fame like the Master.

Some people criticize Tzu Chi volunteers for always wearing a uniform of blue shirt and white pants, and for setting up the Tzu Chi flag whenever they assist others. The critics assume Tzu Chi members are showing off, never realizing that they do this so that those in need can recognize them.

The Master's major concern is how to put people's care and concern for the needy into concrete action; therefore she does not care whether she receives any awards. To her, awards are not as important as the action of helping others. Furthermore, the Master understands that receiving honors creates distraction. Nobel laureate Lee Yuan-tseh, president of Taiwan's Academia Sinica, said that after obtaining the award his originally peaceful life became disquieted and punctuated with troubles and disturbance that came along with the award. These comments allow Tzu Chi members to better understand the Master's insistence on not receiving awards.

32 } *The new community volunteer system*

CHALLENGE: What is the most effective
way to organize volunteers?

"One thousand eyes see the world of suffering
and one thousand hands reach out and help."
MASTER CHENG YEN

Background

Typhoon Herb ravaged Taiwan in 1996 and caused grave damage
to the central and southern areas of the island. Many towns were
flooded, leaving residents stranded on their balconies waiting for
help. Because the water rose so suddenly, many people weren't
prepared and didn't know what to do. The floods also damaged
transportation routes, so it took rescuers a long time to reach
flood victims.

When the first groups of Tzu Chi rescuers arrived, they heard
many people complaining, "Why did the Tzu Chi people come so
late?" This question shook Master Cheng Yen severely and reaf-
firmed her belief that promptness was the most critical factor in
doing rescue work. That Tzu Chi members had missed the first
crucial moment because they were hindered by traffic and other
uncontrollable factors was a problem that couldn't be ignored. She
wondered, "What if the residents of the disaster areas could also

have been mobilized to help?" She realized that if Tzu Chi had commissioners living in every community, they would have been able to organize people and carry out rescue work more quickly. Further still, "It would be a lot better if those people waiting for help on their balconies could have prepared beforehand and cooperated with local Tzu Chi groups. Only when refugees themselves can go into action first can the rescue work become efficient and valid in the shortest possible time."

The knowledge gained from Typhoon Herb prompted the Master to make major changes to the foundation's organizational structure. Originally, senior commissioners led their friends or relatives, who might live in different areas of the country. However, a new pattern was instituted, based on commissioners leading members who live in the same residential community. This new unit became the basic building block for a Tzu Chi community volunteer network that reaches deep into every corner of Taiwan.

Challenge
This reorganization caused much psychological torment for many commissioners. Whereas the original groups were based on commissioners' friends or relatives who knew each other well and could be mobilized very easily, the new units were made up of local residents, many of whom didn't even know each other. It became very difficult for the commissioners to promote Tzu Chi ideology among their neighbors, and many felt that their Tzu Chi "family" had been torn apart. It was hard for a lot of members to adjust to the new system, and the change posed a great challenge to the cohesion of the Tzu Chi commissioners.

With the reorganization, some communities suddenly had many senior commissioners, but some ended up with only one or two. For example, Commissioner Lin Yueh-yun had previously led hundreds of commissioners, but now she was the only commissioner in her community. That meant she had to start again, promoting Tzu Chi with the most basic activities, such as environmental protection. Many senior commissioners say frankly that they still can't get used to the new system.

Although the majority of commissioners weren't too pleased about the reorganization, they agreed to try it out because they respected and believed in the Master's good judgment and supported her idea of bringing Tzu Chi services directly to the communities in the fastest way. Nevertheless, no one was sure that the change would indeed bring better results. Fortunately, when more recent devastating disasters have hit, Tzu Chi members have mobilized quickly and efficiently to reach the affected areas in the shortest time, and Tzu Chi members concede that it is all because of this new network.

Effects and Reflections
Such a huge reorganization was like a major operation for the foundation. The Master was taking a great risk, so how did she ensure success?

First, she matched the goal and the method. Tzu Chi holds tenets such as "Great mercy to strangers and great compassion for all" and "Give joy and relieve suffering, help the poor, and educate the rich," which call for urgent relief for the needy. When the Master realized that Tzu Chi couldn't provide timely assistance when people needed it the most, she realigned the foundation's organizational structure to better meet this goal.

Second, the Master deciphered the warning: a complaint repeated by a commissioner in a casual way was enough to set the

Master thinking. She recognized the urgency of the situation and all the features of the problem. Then she started reorganizing the whole system.

Third, she emphasized a closely knit arrangement. In a huge organization like Tzu Chi, good communication is critical to mobilize its members in a timely manner. By using this strength of numbers, the Master's thorough logic, her communication skills, and her experience in interactions could more easily be transmitted to ensure the vitality of the organization.

The support from within the organization as well as from the public helped Tzu Chi to grow and implement the new community volunteer system. It is like a system of newly planned roads that cover every corner of Taiwan. Whenever there is a need, the network comes alive, spreading the word to the grassroots level, so that neighboring communities can respond and support each other as required. In this way, the foundation is able to mobilize people more powerfully, act more responsively, and function more effectively.

The new network also encourages residents to understand the importance of watching out for their neighborhood. And it transforms individuals. Since community residents now know that a neighbor is a Tzu Chi member, they observe him or her closely. Consequently, volunteers pay special attention to their actions and words. Gradually, they speak more gently and act more properly. These changes may come from pressure from other people at the very beginning, but after some time the inner self will be transformed accordingly, lending support to the saying "Your proper behavior will enhance your inner cultivation."

Every Tzu Chi member has learned something from this new system. For example, one senior commissioner said that when she was "demoted" from district chief to local commissioner, she learned to put her seniority aside, humble herself, and become at ease with the new situation.

The community volunteer network cultivates the spirit of mutual help and solidarity in times of need.

five

WORLDWIDE PROJECTS

33 } *The Tzu Chi international network*

CHALLENGE: How does one grow an organization globally?

"Standing on foreign soil, walking under a foreign sky,
enjoying the social resources of a foreign people, we
should repay their kindness and thus gain their respect."
MASTER CHENG YEN

Background

When my family was preparing to immigrate to Canada, we went
to bid a reluctant farewell to Master Cheng Yen. We told her
that there would not be as many chances to devote our time and
energies to the Tzu Chi missions after we moved to Canada. We
could not help feeling sad and uncertain. The Master, however,
spoke as joyfully to us as she usually did: "Since you are immi-
grating to Canada, why not take Tzu Chi's seed of goodness with
you to your new home? Tzu Chi is like a pure stream that can
flow through five continents. No matter where you are, you can
continue to fulfill the Tzu Chi missions." And so my wife and I
moved to Canada with new hope. A year later, we set up a Tzu
Chi overseas branch office in Vancouver, and we started to plant
the seed of Great Love in a foreign land.

Without any systematic plan, Tzu Chi overseas branches
have opened one by one since 1985. In 1989, Brother Stephen

Huang established the U.S. branch in southern California. Since then, Tzu Chi members have spread the message of Great Love from Taiwan to every corner of the world, setting up branches on five continents. Now, Tzu Chi has 169 overseas offices in forty countries.

Challenge

Tzu Chi overseas branches are not formally part of Master Cheng Yen's plan, nor is the internationalization of Tzu Chi. In fact, the overseas offices are voluntarily set up by local Tzu Chi people.

When the overseas branches are founded, the Master does not supply any financial help. She only gives us her advice: "Be self-sufficient and obtain your resources locally." All overseas branches are developed gradually, building upon the local residents' affiliations with Tzu Chi and the efforts of people with the same ideals.

There are no inflexible rules. All rules are set according to the local culture and social needs and are in conformity with the Tzu Chi spirit. Because of this, all overseas branches have their own distinguishing features and more easily win local recognition and support.

In Canada, for example, we donate money to the local food bank to buy and distribute fresh food to impoverished families every month. We regularly visit nursing homes in Vancouver to cook meals and chat with the elderly. We assisted Meals on Wheels, another charity organization, to deliver food to lonely senior citizens needing assistance.

Effects and Reflections

Many immigrants to foreign countries drift about like duckweed, with no roots, unable to blend into the mainstream of local life.

Before my family left Taiwan, the Master told us that since we would be standing on foreign soil, walking under a foreign sky, and enjoying the social resources of another people, we should repay their kindness. Then we would earn their respect. I took these words to heart, and when I arrived in Canada I became actively involved in local charity work. Not only have I gained inexpressible happiness and satisfaction, I have won the locals' friendship and respect, and thus truly have been able to establish roots in this country. Every time we help the staff at the food bank distribute food to destitute people, it is gratifying to have them tell us that working with Tzu Chi volunteers is a most joyful experience because we are always smiling and friendly.

More and more, I hear stories of how Tzu Chi members have made a difference around the world. In 1992, for example, a race riot broke out in Los Angeles following the acquittal of four police officers involved in beating Rodney King, an African-American who had resisted arrest. During the unrest, some Asian businesses were burned and looted in retaliation for perceived discrimination against African-Americans. A Tzu Chi member, who was from Kaohsiung but living in the United States, was driving down a street when she was intercepted by a group of African-Americans. She was afraid that she would be harmed. While she was mentally preparing herself for a conflict, one of them asked her, "Are you a Korean, Japanese, or Chinese?" She nervously replied, "I'm a Chinese from Taiwan!" Unexpectedly, the group calmed down, instructed her to go straight home, and showed her the best way to leave the area safely! Later, an African-American friend explained that the group was grateful to the Tzu Chi U.S. branch for its help and care for impoverished African-Americans. They would not harm the Chinese.

Similarly, in 1996, Africans from different tribes in Lady-smith, South Africa, decided to adopt the Tzu Chi spirit of Great Love, which transcends races and borders. They put down their weapons, ended the racial and political conflict, and held a candle-light vigil for peace to express their thanks for the friendship and inspiration that Tzu Chi people had given them.

And when a massive earthquake rocked Taiwan on September 21, 1999, Tzu Chi members received much support when raising funds locally. In Canada, a drifter gave us five packs of instant noodles. He told us that he did not have any money, but the instant noodles had been given to him, and he wanted to donate them to help the earthquake survivors in Taiwan. Another man stopped and hugged us to show his care and concern. Other people simply joined in the fundraising activities. The disaster in Taiwan linked Canadian and Taiwanese hearts.

Helping the needy has not only earned Taiwanese immigrants the respect of locals, but their involvement in Tzu Chi work has also helped many of them become happier and more self-confident. For example, a Taiwanese woman living in Canada was depressed and dissatisfied because she was separated from her husband (who was still living and working in Taiwan). Her attitude changed completely after she joined Tzu Chi. When she was working at the food bank distributing food to the needy she saw many people who could barely feed themselves three meals a day. With a sigh of relief she admitted how blessed she was, and for the first time she appreciated how hard her husband was working to provide for the family. Since then, she has never again complained about the separation from her husband. She is grateful for the choice to be a "giver," not a "recipient."

The Master has often said that the reason for carrying out the Tzu Chi missions is to help the poor and educate the rich: we help the poor to overcome their hardships, and we teach the rich to be content and cherish their blessings by helping others. All Tzu Chi people, especially those who reside in foreign nations, hope to spread the spirit of Great Love to every corner of the world and to break down the barriers between different races. At the same time, working with the foundation to aid others helps soothe the lonely hearts of these immigrants and builds their self-confidence and self-respect.

34 } *Providing relief and spreading goodwill worldwide*

CHALLENGE: How can one make a
difference around the world?

"Once born into this world, all people are our
brothers and sisters, even though we do not share
the same parents. Whenever there are disasters
in the world, we should offer as much help as we can."
MASTER CHENG YEN

Background
The year 1991 was a memorable one for Tzu Chi. The organization was making great progress in carrying out its four major missions: charity, medical care, educational development, and cultural promotion. Although Tzu Chi had several overseas branches, most of its energy was focused locally and in Taiwan. When floods ravaged Bangladesh in April 1991, members of the Tzu Chi U.S. branch reported the news to Master Cheng Yen in Taiwan and began to collect donations to help the survivors. The Master immediately called upon Taiwanese children to put aside their daily snack money to help Bangladeshi children. Within one month, Tzu Chi had collected about US$150,000 and handed it over to the Red Cross to help rebuild Bangladesh.

Providing financial assistance to Bangladesh was the beginning of Tzu Chi's international relief work, although the organization's first hands-on mission outside of Taiwan was in Mongolia. This arid country adjacent to the former Soviet Union had depended on Russia and Eastern Europe for long-term political and economic aid. Radical changes in Eastern Europe and the collapse of the Soviet Union in 1989 led to the withdrawal of that aid, and Mongolia soon suffered from serious shortages of machines, tools, and technical personnel. This resulted in a lack of daily goods, and the life of the Mongolian people became mired in difficulties.

In August 1992, the Master received a distress call from the president of the Mongolian Red Cross Society, and she promptly learned all she could about the situation. Later in the year, as living conditions in Mongolia grew worse, the prime minister of Mongolia appealed to many countries for help. At that time, Tzu Chi officially sent a fact-finding team to the country. As soon as the team members returned home, they started planning the relief project. On New Year's Day of the following year, Tzu Chi volunteers returned to Mongolia to distribute relief goods directly to those in need, including medications, food, jackets, blankets, and other items that would keep the victims warm.

Challenge
International relief is another milestone of the Tzu Chi charity mission. Although she had never undertaken the task of providing assistance internationally, the Master grasped the importance of understanding the whole picture before taking action. This is the same principle she applies before setting foot in any new territory. The Master also set the operative norms for international relief work:

1. Directness: Tzu Chi people insist on personally distributing relief goods to those in need, so that the recipients may experience the love and care of Tzu Chi people. This also saves time and prevents any resources from going to waste.

2. Priority: Since resources are limited, Tzu Chi members focus their efforts on the hardest-hit disaster regions and help the people who need assistance the most, so that they can be relieved of their suffering as soon as possible.

3. Respect: Tzu Chi members must always respect local customs and practices, helping others as their friends with an attitude that is neither servile nor supercilious.

4. Pragmatism: The more effort Tzu Chi members contribute, the more people they help. Any unnecessary waste should be avoided. For example, in the relief action in Mongolia, all relief supplies were purchased and manufactured in China to save unnecessary transportation costs. Similarly, after floods in Nepal in 1993, Tzu Chi people designed new houses and planned communities, but contracted local construction companies to do the actual work. Only periodically did Tzu Chi people supervise the work.

Effects and Reflections

Taiwan has no diplomatic relations with many of the countries in which major natural disasters occur; however, the spirit of charity—what Tzu Chi calls its Great Love—extends beyond political borders.

In the fifties and sixties, when Taiwan's social and industrial environments were still developing, the country received aid from the Red Cross and many other international organizations. Now that its living conditions and economic situation have improved and its population is more educated, Tzu Chi members living in Taiwan are able to help others and care for disaster victims elsewhere. As they reciprocate the aid they received, they express their appreciation and demonstrate that we are family living in a global village.

Great Love transcends all boundaries. No matter what our circumstances or where we live, every one of us can help the needy by respecting all life and saving all living beings. Our world will then be compassionate and warm, and our lives will be rich and colorful.

35 } *Responding quickly to the effects of Hurricane Katrina*

CHALLENGE: Are small acts of kindness enough
to heal the damage of immense devastation?

"Where there is a kind heart, there are blessings.
Where there is commitment, there is strength."

MASTER CHENG YEN

Background

At the end of August 2005, one of the deadliest hurricanes in
U.S. history, Katrina, swept along the Gulf Coast of the United
States, leveling homes, leaving hundreds of thousands of people
displaced, and claiming the lives of more than 1,800 people. The
cataclysmic storm caused an estimated US$81 billion worth of
property damage, making it the costliest natural disaster in the
country's history.

The Tzu Chi Foundation immediately mobilized hundreds
of volunteers in response to the aftermath of Hurricane Katrina
and helped evacuees who had been relocated to Texas, Arizona,
Kansas, New York, and California. With so many left homeless, Tzu Chi volunteers supplied hurricane victims with shelter,
food, and other basic necessities. Master Cheng Yen urged Tzu
Chi volunteers around the world to help families recover from this
disaster as quickly as possible.

Challenge

"I feel an indescribable sense of pain and sorrow," the Master said to all Tzu Chi members in a notice regarding the state of emergency in the regions affected by Katrina. Tzu Chi needed to help—that was obvious. The only question was, could help arrive fast enough?

"The role of global warming cannot be denied, as scientific studies tell us," the Master told Tzu Chi members. "The disasters nowadays are increasingly more severe, and in the future, given human beings' wayward activities, the disasters will become even more devastating. The small acts here and there may seem minor, but very quickly we find upon us a calamity that tears apart families and destroys cities. As a member of this global village, how can we remain apart and take no action?"

All Tzu Chi members from around the world responded to the Master's urgent call. With free transportation provided by Taiwan's China Airlines, Tzu Chi shipped 10,818 boxes containing medical pouches to Los Angeles, where Tzu Chi volunteers distributed the supplies to hurricane victims and low-income patients. In addition, Tzu Chi set up a database to collect information on missing people to serve the Chinese community and other evacuees in a systematic way.

Tzu Chi also provided immediate and direct financial assistance to Katrina evacuees in the form of emergency checks or gift cards, which helped families pay for daily necessities. Affected families also received a prepaid thirty-minute phone card and a letter from Master Cheng Yen. In the letter, the Master said to the evacuees: "Besides helping you to meet needs, we hope the aid that we give can also be a source of comfort and support to you—knowing that it contains the love and good wishes of people around the world. These supplies will one day be used up, but we hope the love they hold in them will always stay with you. Today, our volunteers are there in person to represent the love and good wishes from people around the globe. Living on this planet, we are all connected to one another."

Tzu Chi volunteers set up a table at an evacuee shelter in Beaumont, Texas, to accept applications for the relief package. At first, many disaster victims swarmed in front of the table. One policeman instructed the crowd to form a line and said: "You need to appreciate! In coming here, they [Tzu Chi volunteers] provide care and love, asking for nothing in return. They don't need to take pressure like this. Please be thoughtful and thankful." Those words proved to be effective. As a result, everyone lined up in an orderly fashion.

Tzu Chi volunteers were instructed to give out the relief package with both hands while saying "thank you" to demonstrate respect, gratitude, and love. The evacuees were not considered as refugees but as neighbors struggling through a difficult time.

The Tzu Chi relief team was, however, presented with some administrative challenges. Volunteers discovered that some of the evacuees tried to acquire multiple gift cards by sending different family members to the relief office. To ensure relief aid would be distributed fairly, volunteers tracked identification records. The Master also instructed that each family should receive an amount capped at US$200.

In the end, Tzu Chi committed over US$4 million for emergency relief efforts in the region. Tzu Chi Canada was able to provide US$1 million within a week. Members in over forty countries also responded quickly to the call of the Master to raise funds to support ongoing and subsequent relief plans. As of spring 2008, Tzu Chi had given more than US$4,120,458 in financial assistance to Katrina evacuees. More than 22,487 families—58,553 people—received Tzu Chi's emergency cash gift in the form of a check, gift card, or debit card. Each family received an average of $200. More than one thousand Tzu Chi volunteers have participated in the relief effort.

Effects and Reflections

The Master says: "We should have a gracious mindset when serving as volunteers, for only a volunteer who is grateful can be happy. Real gratitude is portrayed through our actions."

Among the evacuees we served, I particularly remember a young American woman. She told me that she had been traveling to many countries but was now stranded by Hurricane Katrina. She had been staying in a stadium in Houston with five thousand other evacuees for two weeks. Her greatest hardship, though, was being separated from her son, who suffered from asthma and could not stay in such a crowded place, so had to stay somewhere else. She missed her child terribly, but she had no money to go to see him. She felt she was not taking good care of him and was saddened by this thought.

We bowed and presented to her, with both hands, the US$200 cash. We explained to her that it embodied multiple blessings from hundreds of our members, who sent their best wishes along with the money. Our members were all hoping that her hardship and that of many others would be over soon. This young woman was noticeably moved.

"For the first time [in weeks] you put a smile on my face," she said. It seemed that her worries were gone just like that. I could see her face light up. I'll never forget that sight for as long as I live. When we bring happiness to people, we also bring happiness to ourselves.

36 } *Transcending political differences in China*

CHALLENGE: How does one overcome
long-term mistrust to create good?

"When others hurt, we feel the pain; when others suffer,
we feel the sorrow. Let us step across political boundaries
and spread the true Great Love in our hearts."
MASTER CHENG YEN

Background

In May 1991, flooding on an unprecedented scale struck central
and eastern China. Floodwaters destroyed riverbanks, swallowed
up houses and farmland, and washed away livestock in nineteen
provinces. Thousands of survivors were left homeless and forced
to build temporary shacks on higher ground.

Master Cheng Yen saw the televised news broadcasts. When
she thought about such a large number of flood victims living
without food just across the Taiwan Strait, she could not bring
herself to swallow even a bite of her own food. The Tzu Chi U.S.
branch office sent a fax a few days later stating, "People here are
worried about the Chinese flood victims. Everyone wishes to
donate money and provide emergency relief via Tzu Chi. We are
all waiting for your instructions." The Master could not call for
immediate action. With more than fifty years of political tensions

between China and Taiwan and with a law barring the preaching of Buddhism in China, no one knew whether or not Chinese officials would accept Tzu Chi's relief aid.

Challenge

The question of whether Tzu Chi could, or should, provide relief aid to mainland China tested the Master's courage and wisdom. Within the foundation, some members approved and some disapproved.

Once again, the Master showed her extraordinary wisdom. First, she explored the viewpoints of both the Taiwanese authorities and the Chinese authorities. Once she understood the positions of both sides on the matter, she obtained their approval to begin relief work. Then she zealously started surveying the disaster areas and planning rescue and aid activities. As she explained her decision to conduct relief work in China, she emphasized that the Buddha taught us to treat all human beings as equals and with unconditional kindness and compassion.

Despite the fact that people often transferred the political confrontations and disputes into their daily lives, and some questioned whether a Taiwan-based organization should be doing relief work in China, the Master completely overlooked these doubts. After all, the flood victims were innocent, and saving people should always be the priority. Tzu Chi's key value is "Great mercy even to strangers, and great compassion for all." To most effectively carry out its mission of providing relief, Tzu Chi summarized its intent with a few guidelines:

1. One objective: To give the flood victims in the disaster areas enough supplies to tide them over until spring.

2. Two principles:
   Directness—To show the care of Tzu Chi people, all relief goods and materials must be handed directly to the victims.

   Priority—The worst-affected, most critical disaster regions should be helped first.

3. Three "no's": There should be no talk about politics, propaganda, or Buddhism.

4. Four types of relief provisions: Tzu Chi would provide medical supplies, food for three to six months, clothes to protect the victims against cold, and money.

Several Tzu Chi members then traveled to China to assess firsthand which areas most needed aid and what the foundation could provide. When the fact-finding team presented Tzu Chi's guidelines on relief to the Chinese officials, they replied, "Exactly how much are you going to donate? Why not just donate money for the relief goods, and give it to the authorities to do the overall planning?"

Even more difficult was that both the authorities and the public doubted Tzu Chi's intentions: *Were they sent by the Nationalist Party to spy on us? Maybe these people are using religion to mask some political objectives.*

Tzu Chi people were not discouraged. The Master had told us before we left for China, "You are going to 'beseech' them to let us do relief work, so you shall respect others and be polite when you communicate with them. If their opinions are different from ours, you shall try your best to persuade them and to complete the mission with perfection."

The first meeting was a failure, but the fact-finding team

returned to their hotel and waited for another opportunity. Finally, an official showed his willingness to cooperate, and after much rational and peaceful dialogue, the authorities began to understand Tzu Chi's conduct and ideals and changed their attitudes. A common consensus was finally reached.

The fact-finding team first went to Anhui Province to survey the effects of the floods, and then they drafted the first relief plan. They requested that local authorities gather data on the required amount of food, clothes, medicine, and money and the number of houses needed by flood victims. In addition, the team decided that Tzu Chi members could help fix or rebuild welfare houses, rest homes, schools, and hospitals.

After completing their assessment and forming concrete resolutions, the Tzu Chi fact-finding team returned to Taipei and gave their recommendations to the Master. After listening to their reports, the Master said to the commissioners and the Honorary Board members, "Inside one grain of rice, the sun and moon are hidden; inside a half-liter pot, mountains and rivers are cooked." This means that unlimited love comes from the limited resources Tzu Chi provides, and this love will go on forever.

Under the Master's direction, foundation members hit the streets to collect donations, and they held a charity bazaar at National Taiwan University. Touched by the Tzu Chi spirit of Great Love, many people donated money. With these donations, Tzu Chi's relief work in China officially began.

In the process of the relief work, everyone stood firmly by the rule, "Each donation is to be spent only according to the purpose specified by the donor." Therefore, all the members of the relief team paid for their own plane tickets and travel expenses.

While we were in China, all Tzu Chi members kept the

Master's exhortations firmly in mind: with grateful hearts, treat the flood victims as family; share happiness and pain with them; abide by the Ten Precepts and pay attention to our manners; and maintain a vegetarian diet, since vegetarian food is easier to prepare, more sanitary, and more humble. The Tzu Chi volunteers painstakingly distributed the relief goods directly to the victims, giving without demanding anything in return. Our sincerity touched the local authorities and melted their indifferent hearts; one after another, these officials joined in the relief work.

Everything Tzu Chi people did in China was not just for the purpose of settling the victims' present problems, but also to renew their hope. Tzu Chi people built two-floor reinforced concrete houses for refugees, and once these were completed, many people saw a positive future ahead of them. In an unprecedented move, Chinese officials even issued ownership certificates to the flood survivors for the Tzu Chi houses.

Effects and Reflections
The relief work for the flood victims in central and eastern China was significant in three ways. First, the process became an excellent model for future Tzu Chi relief work in China. Second, the Chinese felt the care and concern from Taiwan, were able to put their political differences aside, and recognized the good faith between the two peoples. Last, the floods in China were important tests for Tzu Chi's Buddhist precepts and teachings. By overcoming all the difficulties both from within and outside the Tzu Chi organization, members truly practiced the Tzu Chi spirit of "treating all beings as our family and equals, helping all suffering beings."

Jesus Christ once said, "You shall love your neighbor as yourself," and "Those who say 'I love God' and hate their brothers or sisters are liars; for those who do not love the brothers and sisters whom they have seen, cannot love God whom they have not seen." The *Wonderful Lotus Sutra* states that the Buddha treated all living beings as equals with his compassionate heart.

37 } *Reconciliation along a once-damaged river*

CHALLENGE: How can environmental
cleanup ease human relations?

"The love of a bodhisattva is like a glass of water.
It is clean and colorless. You can see all the way
through it from the very top to the very bottom.
It is a love as pure as clean water."
MASTER CHENG YEN

Background

Indonesia's Kali Angke River was once notorious for being "the
black heart of Jakarta." The extremely polluted body of water was
filthy and smelly. Yet, tens of thousands of people—many from
rural areas who were looking for a better life in the city—lived
along the riverbanks in huts and depended on the Kali Angke as
their main water source.

A young man and his wife had lived here for twelve years after
moving from a rural village in central Java. The couple had a small
manufacturing shop along the river, which was also their home.
Over time, they had become numb to the ugly, foul-smelling scene.
The only thing they feared was the regular flooding that happened
every year.

When asked if they would throw garbage into the river themselves, the wife replied without hesitation, "Of course! Everyone is doing that, why shouldn't we?"

Knowing that this was the mentality of residents, observers weren't surprised to see items such as furniture flowing slowly downstream, along with the dead bodies of cats, dogs, and chickens. The river was so packed with discarded bottles that people could make a living—though not a decent one—by collecting them from the water every day.

People living upstream used Kali Angke water to flush their toilets, brush their teeth, and wash their hands. Residents downstream used this same water to wash their clothes and even to rinse their rice.

The Kali Angke, located northwest of Jakarta, also carries with it a long history of ethnic conflict between the indigenous Indonesians and the Chinese Indonesians. In 1740, it was said there were so many Chinese being killed that one could get across the river by stepping on their floating corpses. In fact, the river's name refers to this legacy: Kali Angke is Indonesian for "Red River."

The relationship between the Indonesians and the Chinese has never been a peaceful one. Massive, nationwide anti-Chinese riots were frequent in Indonesia—from the 1960s through to the 1990s. The Chinese accounted for just 4 percent of the population but they controlled the country's retail economy. Out of this imbalance grew a hatred toward the Chinese, who were denied citizenship, even if they had lived there for their entire lives. Celebrating Chinese festivals was prohibited, and Chinese signs and publications were banned. Children learning the Chinese language could not do so publicly.

Adding to this tension, the Indonesians were Muslim while many of the Chinese were Christian.

Challenge

In January 2002, Jakarta suffered a huge flood. The Kali Angke engulfed the badly built huts along the banks and threatened the already destitute lives of the locals. Millions of people were affected and tens of thousands were displaced.

Tzu Chi responded immediately by offering medical supplies and other relief materials, as well as free clinical services. After the floods receded, villagers, the military, and local Tzu Chi volunteers carried out several huge cleanup campaigns. In late September 2002, the Jakarta government sent out five excavators and dug out tons of garbage from the river and the riverbanks. Tzu Chi was determined to restore the Kali Angke. The plan was to divide the cleanup of the river into three parts: north, central, and south. To solve the flooding problem once and for all, embankments would be built. New trees would be planted, and a park would be built to create more open space for the residents.

One young man whose livelihood depended on the river's accumulation of plastic bottles was excited to hear that the river would be cleaned up. When asked if he was worried about losing his income, he optimistically said: "I'm more than happy to look for another job!"

Moreover, Tzu Chi wanted to help people living in illegally built riverside huts relocate to modern living complexes with clinics, schools, and other accompanying facilities. Tzu Chi's ambitious plan was to reshape the character of the whole community, hoping that by devoting their love and care to the local Indonesians, the ethnic conflict between them and the Chinese would one day become a thing of the past.

In November 2002, that dream came closer to being realized. Flags of the Tzu Chi Foundation flew over crowds of around six thousand people on both sides of the Kali Angke. A dragon boat race, involving both Chinese and Indonesians, was being held on that once-foul river.

Six boats dashed out from the starting line at the stroke of a gong. Although the river water was still black, the dragon boats sailed along without impediment from floating garbage. That was a scene no one could have imagined a year before.

But the Tzu Chi spirit didn't stop there. Volunteers and local entrepreneurs went on to build a "Tzu Chi Great Love Village" for the poverty-stricken residents. Here people could live clean, healthy lives, their children could go to school, and the elderly could access health care at the local clinic.

Tzu Chi Cengkarang Village, north of Jakarta, occupies over five hectares of land. The village consists of 55 five-story buildings, including 1,100 family units. The Indonesian government provided the land, and all the construction costs were raised by Tzu Chi volunteers in Indonesia.

Effects and Reflections

It was with great joy that Tzu Chi, through relief work, found a starting point for mending the damaged relations between local Indonesians and Chinese Indonesians.

Today, the Indonesian government, not just the country's Chinese population, celebrates the Chinese New Year. Little red posters bearing the phrase "Kung Hey Fat Choy" (or, "wishing you fortune," a traditional new year's greeting) are distributed and posted.

Kali Angke used to be the geographic focal point of centuries of bloody conflicts. Just as the river was prone to overflow, the violence between these two peoples frequently spread across the country. Tzu Chi's dedication to clean up the ugly river and restore its natural beauty, as well as Tzu Chi's subsequent effort in building affordable housing for the residents, has altered—for the better—the Indonesian impression of the Chinese. Tzu Chi's efforts have helped heal wounds that are centuries old.

38 } *Establishing an Asian bone marrow registry*

CHALLENGE: How can one give the gift of life?

"You can save a life without harming yourself. We are
looking for a person, and that person might be you! "
MASTER CHENG YEN

Background

In 1992, Wen Wen-ling, a Taiwanese student who was studying
in the United States, was diagnosed with leukemia, a blood disease characterized by an abnormally high white blood cell count.
A bone marrow transplant was her only hope for survival. Since
bone marrow, the connective tissue found in the cavity of most
bones, is closely connected to one's genetic makeup, the success
rate of nonrelative donations is extremely low. As there were no
compatible donors in the U.S. bone marrow data bank, Wen
asked the Tzu Chi U.S. branch for help, hoping to find a compatible donor among the numerous Tzu Chi members of Taiwanese
descent.

The U.S. branch immediately held several blood-testing drives,
but unfortunately, no compatible donor was found. Tzu Chi
members in the US then appealed to their counterparts in Taiwan,
hoping that Wen could improve her chances of finding a successful match in this small country with its closely related population.

Challenge

At the time of the request, the concept of bone marrow donation was still known to only a handful of people in Taiwan. Because of her incomplete understanding of the effects of bone marrow donation, Master Cheng Yen was not able to come to any immediate conclusions, but she immediately set to learning about the advantages and disadvantages of bone marrow donations before making a final decision.

The Master questioned specialists and studied related medical documents, since most people believed that donating marrow would cause health problems and sterility. However, after talking with past donors and seeing them with her own eyes, the Master realized that donating bone marrow is not harmful to the donor. She initiated communication with the Department of Health about establishing a bone marrow registry. In September 1993, the Department of Health invited representatives from all the major local hospitals, the Chinese Blood Services Foundation, and the Tzu Chi Foundation to a conference. Everyone elected the Tzu Chi Foundation to establish and operate a bone marrow registry.

Guided by the principle of respect for all life, Tzu Chi members zealously promoted bone marrow donations. Under the meticulous planning of the Tzu Chi commissioners, the first bone marrow registration drive attracted more than four thousand potential marrow donors, about half of whom were Tzu Chi members. The foundation realized that to promote marrow donations, members had to set a good example. If they were afraid to donate their marrow or even to have their blood tested, how could they convince others to do the same?

Tzu Chi commissioners joined with medical personnel in giving presentations in schools, government organizations, and companies to promote the concept of bone marrow donation. Tzu Chi also created two advertisements to popularize this mission. One was a poster of a little girl with leukemia. Her pure, innocent expression touched many hearts worldwide. The other was a television commercial featuring Jackie Chan, the internationally renowned kung fu star, as the voluntary spokesperson. In the ad, Chan rushed anxiously through the streets, then announced: "Tzu Chi and I are looking for someone, and you might be the one!"

Through the hard work of the Tzu Chi commissioners and successful print media and broadcasting promotions, within two years the Tzu Chi Marrow Donor Registry was able to collect data on more than 100,000 potential donors. By January 2008, the number of donors reached 307,657.

Effects and Reflections

Even though the success rate for matching bone marrow donations is low, the data collected is the only hope for patients with blood diseases. In May 1994, the first nonrelative marrow recipient, a boy named Wei Chih-hsiang, received marrow from Yeh Mei-ching, a student at National Taiwan University. The transplant was a success. When the two met a year later (the law prevents donors and recipients from having contact before this time), Wei said excitedly, "Big sister, my life was given by you and the blood that circulates in my body is also from you!" Those present were moved to tears.

Another touching story is that of the campaign poster child, Chi-chi. She is living with both leukemia and Down's syndrome. Chi-chi's mother was not keen to have Chi-chi featured on the poster; however, she finally agreed in order to promote public awareness of bone marrow donation. In fact, the response to the poster was unexpectedly strong. Chi-chi received an outpouring of support from many people. Maybe she was blessed by being the poster child.

By January 31, 2008, Tzu Chi had enabled more than 1,504 successful bone marrow transplants in twenty-six countries. Of these, 442 were in Taiwan, and 1,062 were in other countries such as the United States, Canada, Europe, Australia, Japan, Singapore, Hong Kong, and mainland China. In China, especially in Zhejiang Province, each case was a lead story in the local media, and the transplants helped diffuse the bad feelings between Taiwan and China.

The Tzu Chi Taiwan Marrow Donor Registry has become one of Taiwan's most important contributions to the international medical world. It is the largest in Asia and the fifth-largest in the world, behind the United States and Europe. In terms of population, however, the proportion of volunteer donors is already the highest in the world.

six

HOPE FOR TOMORROW

39 } *Spreading the message of love and compassion in a digital age*

CHALLENGE: How can one most effectively propagate humanitarian ideals?

"A word is like a ferry. We need to properly use this ferry if we wish to reach the other shore of peace and joy. " MASTER CHENG YEN

Background

Master Cheng Yen is a very reserved person who doesn't like to face cameras. In the early years she courteously declined interview requests, and until recently she would only occasionally meet with the press. Similarly, the Tzu Chi Foundation is not very good at traditional media-based public relations, preferring to let the members' actions speak for themselves. Although Tzu Chi now has a public relations department that releases news on special events, it does not have a comprehensive public relations strategy and it does not initiate publicity. Most interviews are pushed forward by enthusiastic members or solicited by the media, and the number of interviews the Master has accepted is small.

However, despite her natural reticence, the Master no longer rejects the idea of being interviewed, and the foundation now uses a variety of technological media to spread its message.

Challenge

How and why has the Master's frame of mind been transformed? Even though the Master believes compassionate action is the most powerful way to propagate the Buddhist dharma, she has never neglected the disseminative power of words. *Tzu Chi Monthly*, the original publication of the Tzu Chi Foundation, was first printed in 1967. At the very beginning, its only purpose was to help the organization earn credibility among donors by enumerating how much money Tzu Chi had raised and from how many people. Later on, this monthly magazine began to report on a variety of Tzu Chi activities and good deeds and propagate the message of goodness, beauty, and truth in the world. The publication gradually became the spiritual food of many Tzu Chi members, educating many people and encouraging them to become more active in humanitarian work.

The publication of the *Tzu Chi Monthly* opened the door to Tzu Chi's mission of cultural promotion. However, as more people joined the organization in doing good works, the magazine's scope was no longer sufficient. Books followed, but Master Cheng Yen gradually recognized that in an age increasingly dominated by mass media, to purify people's minds and to make the world a place of warmth and loving care, it was necessary to make use of technology to disseminate Buddhist thoughts and Tzu Chi spirit.

In 1985, the "Tzu Chi World" radio program was first broadcast. As the truth, beauty, and goodness of the Tzu Chi world were spread across the airwaves, people who were not good at reading could learn about Tzu Chi and attain inner peace by listening to the programs. The transmission speed of radio broadcasts and the universality of radios more than made up for the limits of printed publications.

In 1995, soon after the cable television market was opened in Taiwan, the Master saw that Tzu Chi must make good use of this influential medium to spread the Buddhist spirit. Americans spend almost one-third of their leisure time watching television, and Taiwanese watch about eight hours of programming per day! How influential a medium TV can be! Therefore she asked Huang Ching-wen, then a senior news anchorwoman, to plan the production and broadcast of television programs for Tzu Chi.

It takes a large amount of capital to set up a television station. At that time, the cable television field was highly competitive. A lot of consortiums invested in the technology, but many failed due to insufficient financial resources. In view of this, Ms. Huang came up with a proposal that involved far less risk: instead of a television station, set up a program production center. There were two benefits. First, all the cable stations were in need of programs to fill in their time slots. If Tzu Chi could provide programs for them, thus saving them a lot of production costs, they would surely welcome the cooperation. Second, in addition to transmitting the Tzu Chi spirit, these programs could save Tzu Chi from having to spend a lot of money on the operation of a television station.

The Master agreed to this proposal, which seemed to satisfy all considerations. Thus Tzu Chi embarked on its electronic media endeavor. Cable television stations warmly received the "Tzu Chi World" programs. Beginning on December 1, 1995, the programs were broadcast three times a day on different channels.

With the broadcasts of "Tzu Chi World," Tzu Chi became the first Buddhist organization in Taiwan to air TV shows. In the beginning, we were all excited about the warm response across Taiwan. But as time went on, problems began to surface. The biggest drawback of handing over programs for transmission was that the image of Tzu Chi could not be conveyed in its entirety. Another shortcoming was that the cable stations determined when the shows would be broadcast. Since most television stations are commercially oriented, they often pull programs off the air or change the show time just to win high audience ratings. Furthermore, Tzu Chi did not have the right to decide what programs should precede and follow "Tzu Chi World." If those shows contained violence or sex, the Tzu Chi programs would appear out of place and their effect upon the audience would be greatly reduced. For these reasons, Master Cheng Yen, after serious consideration, decided to establish the Tzu Chi TV station. Broadcasting began on January 1, 1998.

Tzu Chi TV is now operating well. Although high ratings are not its target, it still keeps improving the quality of its programs. Tzu Chi TV emphasizes issues that concern people's livelihood, charitable activities, and Tzu Chi events. This focus sets it apart from the news programs that appear on other channels. In addition, "Tzu Chi Theater" presents inspiring, true stories of Tzu Chi people to both educate and entertain, and it provides viewers who are fond of soap operas with another choice.

Furthermore, Tzu Chi TV allows members to share in shaping and communicating the news. To save operating costs, the station trains its own photography volunteers, inviting those who are interested in film work to carry their own photography equipment and capture good shots for Tzu Chi TV. As well, when there is a lack of staff in the programming and news departments, these volunteers fill in.

Effects and Reflections
In recent years, the *Tzu Chi Monthly* and reporting by other media have made the Tzu Chi spirit and events more widely known,

resulting in more people making special trips to visit the Master. In order to spread Tzu Chi's ideals and spirit, the Master is also more willing to accept media interviews. However, Tzu Chi still hardly ever initiates the interviews. To talk with Master Cheng Yen, reporters generally just accompany her on her island-wide tours. This is because she really has a very tight schedule, and also because she wants the reporters to see for themselves how Tzu Chi people work together.

Although the Master dislikes facing cameras, she speaks to reporters and gives lectures to Tzu Chi members via TV. From these changes, we can see that the Master is determined, but not stubborn. Her spiritual convictions are consistent and her behavior always agrees with the time and space she is in. Through observing the Master's conduct, we realize that to accomplish a great purpose we need to constantly adjust our footsteps and behavior. We must never be complacent with past achievements and habits.

The Master expects the Tzu Chi TV station to record the history of Tzu Chi and bear witness to this era, so that people all over the world can listen to the Master's lectures and see Tzu Chi people's benevolent actions and thoughts. This will provide an unobtrusive way for people to learn about Buddhism and Tzu Chi.

"No matter where you are now," said the Master, "as long as you are willing to turn on the television and set it to the Tzu Chi TV channel, we will walk into your house and introduce the Buddha's teachings to you. The key is whether or not you will open the door to us."

We often hear people criticize today's TV programs for containing violence, vulgarity, and pornography and for the influential role commercials play in them.

Tzu Chi TV makes an effort to reverse this tide; after all, people will never cease to aspire to the good. The swift growth of the numbers of Tzu Chi volunteers and the rapid spread of Tzu Chi ideals and beliefs are guarantees that Tzu Chi TV will continue to make progress and become ever more popular.

The success of this approach can be measured in part by the fact that several organizations have heard and are promoting Tzu Chi's message independently. In Taiwan, many universities, including National Chengchi University, offer courses about Tzu Chi's humanitarian activities. In Canada, *Global Connections: Geography for the 21st Century*, a textbook for secondary school students in the province of Nova Scotia, discusses Master Cheng Yen in a case study about the influence of religious leaders.

40 } *Leading the way in disaster relief operations*

CHALLENGE: How can an organization
mobilize thousands of volunteers instantly?

"It takes not only love, but also method to do good deeds.
Great Love is the driving force behind the deeds of Tzu Chi
people. As for the methods of doing good, we accumulate
our experiences from repeated mistakes." MASTER CHENG YEN

Background

In the early morning of September 21, 1999, violent tremors suddenly shook Taiwan. In complete darkness, Master Cheng Yen got up, turned on the radio, and began to listen to the early reports of the earthquake.

The radio broadcasts consisted of fragmented reports on the damage. The worst catastrophe at that moment was the collapse of the twelve-story Tunghsing Building in Taipei. However, because all the electricity in the western region of the island had been cut off, the extent of the damage in central Taiwan, where the epicenter was located, was still unknown. The unusual stillness made one fear.

The worried Master instructed the nuns at the Abode of Still Thoughts to call the Tzu Chi Hospital, the Yu-Li Hospital, and commissioners all over Taiwan and find out what had happened.

Even though it was 1:50 a.m. when Master Te Jung dialed several numbers and received no responses, Master Cheng Yen knew clearly that something terrible had happened. The Master was on tenterhooks and told everyone around her to keep their cell phones on. In fact, Taiwan had suffered the worst earthquake in its history: the disaster would eventually claim 2,400 lives and leave 8,500 people injured and 10,000 without homes.

Tzu Chi people were already rushing to various disaster areas in northern, central, and southern Taiwan. At 2:00 a.m., barely fifteen minutes after the first big tremor struck, two members who lived nearby arrived at the collapsed Tunghsing Building. Just before 2:00 a.m., the director of general affairs at the Tzu Chi Taichung branch office got on his motorbike and dashed to the office after the violent tremor shook him from his sleep. At the same time, a Tzu Chi member living in Puli hurried to the Puli Christian Hospital. He climbed to the seventh floor and carried patients down the stairs one by one.

In the early morning of September 21, without any commands or instructions from their superiors, Tzu Chi volunteers set up thirty rescue stations around the island. These volunteers were guided only by their compassionate hearts and their accumulated experience in relief operations.

Challenge

In the days following the earthquake, many people asked the Master, "How did you mobilize Tzu Chi members so quickly? How could Tzu Chi be so efficient?" She always gave the same answer: "We didn't mobilize anything at all! What Tzu Chi people have is love, and their abundant love is the driving force that motivates them to go wherever there is suffering."

Although the extent of the damage caused by the quake was not yet clear early on September 21, the Master immediately ordered Tzu Chi volunteers in Taichung and Taipei to withdraw money from their bank accounts. The headquarters in Hualien also set aside $20 million in Taiwanese currency (US$ 65,000) for use as relief funds.

By September 22, news of how seriously the quake had affected the island gradually came to be known, and the damage was unimaginable. While Tzu Chi people were still busily engaged in emergency relief work, the Master was already thinking of post-earthquake reconstruction. She asked members to begin purchasing construction materials for the building of prefabricated houses. At the same time, she also dispatched a medical team from the Hualien Tzu Chi Hospital to the disaster areas and asked members of the Tzu Chi International Medical Association to pitch in to help provide medical aid. On the third day after the earthquake, she went to the disaster sites and personally oversaw the Tzu Chi rescue operations.

After surveying the sites, she first ordered that no Tzu Chi people do anything that would jeopardize their own lives. For example, they were asked not to go to mountainous areas where communications had been cut off. The Master made it clear that Tzu Chi volunteers were backup forces for the regular relief professionals. Rescue work that demanded expertise should be done by professional rescue teams.

The first step Tzu Chi took to help survivors of the earthquake was to dispense US$150 to each household. The guiding principle was that it would be better to give money to the wrong person than not to give money to a real survivor. Thereafter, there were three stages of relief work to do: attend to the physical needs of survivors, provide treatment for mental and emotional trauma, and help those who lost their homes to obtain shelter.

To tend to the physical needs of survivors, Tzu Chi volunteers distributed relief money, clothes, sleeping bags, and comforters and prepared hot meals, so that survivors wouldn't have to suffer from cold and hunger. To alleviate the survivors' trauma, Tzu Chi members provided care and companionship. They held vigils, paid visits to victims' homes, listened to what they had to say, and comforted their wounded hearts. To help survivors obtain shelter, Tzu Chi decided to build prefabricated houses for them. Once those left homeless had a roof over their heads, their hope would be more easily rekindled.

Effects and Reflections
The amazing call to action and great efficiency demonstrated by Tzu Chi people after the September 21 earthquake saved many people. The reason the foundation was able to respond so quickly and effectively was because of the Tzu Chi community volunteer network and the relief distribution drills and international relief work that Tzu Chi people had taken part in previously. Members had gained experience from small community activities as well as large-scale international relief operations. Were it not for these opportunities for participation and the repeated reviews after every event, it would have been quite impossible to achieve such rapid mobilization and great efficiency.

Master Cheng Yen always reminds those who take part in relief work to look after themselves: "Your safety is my life. To save other people, you first need to take good care of yourselves." In addition to asking that Tzu Chi volunteers not risk their lives in any way, she also requested roll calls every night after the volunteers returned from the disaster sites, to ensure that no one had gotten lost.

Despite these precautions, a Tzu Chi volunteer was delivering relief supplies to remote mountain areas. On his way back, a tree suddenly fell across the road ahead of him, leaving just a narrow lane through which he could pass. For a moment he could not decide whether to drive forward or stay put. When he instinctively stopped his car, a huge rock tumbled down the mountain and carried the tree down into the deep valley. Greatly shocked, he looked back and saw more than ten cars behind him. He felt extremely relieved and lucky because his choice had saved many lives. When he related the episode to the Master, she said with a sigh, "That's why I'm here—to pull you back a little so that you won't dash into danger or get yourself into trouble!" Although more than a hundred thousand Tzu Chi members participated in the earthquake relief work, no one was reported injured.

What Tzu Chi did for survivors of the September 21 earthquake won a lot of praise, but there was also criticism of how Tzu Chi people took pleasure in being in the spotlight. Actually, it was not our intention to do the government's work, but to support the professionals. When other organizations could take over Tzu Chi's work, members moved on to fill another need.

Many people criticized the government for being inefficient, especially compared with Tzu Chi and other private organizations. Nongovernmental organizations have more freedom in doing things, however, so of course they can respond more quickly. In the end, be it the government, Tzu Chi, or other private organizations, our invaluable experiences can only be accumulated day by day. We should all review what we have done before and see if there is still room for improvement. In this way we can all improve ourselves.

41 } *Building villages around the world*

CHALLENGE: How can one create
community in the wake of disaster?

"If victims of the September 21 earthquake cannot
obtain shelter, it will be hard for them to attain peace
of mind. We should try our best to provide them
with shelter so that they won't plunge into depression."
MASTER CHENG YEN

Background

The September 21, 1999, earthquake destroyed more than ten
thousand buildings in Taiwan. Many people were forced to put
up tents on the ravaged ground. Taking refuge under thin tarpau-
lins, they longed for a home.

The government provided help for survivors in two ways:
they could either apply for "rent subsidies" of US$100 and use
the money to rent a house, or they could move into prefabricated
modular houses built by the government and private charitable
organizations. The Tzu Chi Foundation was one of the organizations that decided to help build prefabricated modular houses.

These temporary living quarters, which are packed in boxes
and can be easily set up by volunteers, can also be repacked after
use for the next relief work. Also, Tzu Chi designed construction
that was appropriate for the local conditions. For instance, the

buildings built by Tzu Chi in Iran after it suffered a devastating earthquake in December 2003 were structurally designed by our engineers to withstand future quakes. They are built to stand for hundreds of years.

Challenge

Although the prefabricated houses were meant to be temporary shelters, the first thought that entered Master Cheng Yen's mind was: What kind of houses would the survivors like to move into? She wanted them to feel at home.

After some deliberation, she summed up a few key points:

1. The prefabricated houses should be located close to the collapsed homes. Some earthquake survivors opted for the prefabricated house because they knew that it would not be easy to find suitable houses for rent; more importantly, others just did not want to leave their homes. If Tzu Chi could build houses near the disaster areas, reasoned the Master, it would fall more in line with the wishes of the victims.

2. The houses should be spacious. Originally, the government designed prefabricated houses of about twenty-six square meters (280 sq ft), following the style of the temporary shelters built in Kobe, Japan, after the Hanshin earthquake in 1995. But the Master insisted that the houses Tzu Chi built should be forty square meters (430 sq ft), with three rooms and a bathroom, thinking that if the houses were too cramped, the survivors might more keenly feel like victims and consequently be unable to muster enough strength to plan for their future.

3. The houses should be strong, durable, and environmentally friendly. Even though the houses were only temporary shelters,

the building materials should still be strong enough to withstand earthquakes and typhoons in case another earthquake hit. Consequently, the houses were raised off the ground to enable the soil beneath them to dry more easily and the moisture in the houses to dissipate more quickly.

WITH THE HELP of 180,000 volunteers, the Tzu Chi prefabricated houses were finished very quickly—on average, one village was completed every ten days. Participants included executives of big enterprises as well as street peddlers. Some of them laid bricks and some of them built walls. The Master often says, "With more people come more strength and blessings," and with the participation of so many people, the construction work progressed quickly. Those who pitched in to help felt deeply the happiness of giving. By the end of November 1999, a total of 1,700 prefabricated houses had been built. Every brick and tile of each house carried the love of numerous people. To create a sense of community, a public meeting place was included in every village so that inhabitants could interact with and support each other.

Tzu Chi volunteers did not stop caring for survivors of the earthquake after the houses were finished. When survivors moved into the newly constructed houses, Tzu Chi people not only helped them move, but also gave them all sorts of household appliances and articles as presents. Some of the presents, such as gas stoves, thermos bottles, curtains, and newspapers, were donated by people all around Taiwan; others, such as dining utensils, blankets, and comforters, were specially purchased by Tzu Chi members. These gifts were not expensive but they were proof of people's concern for the victims. In recognition of the love and warmth that went into building the homes and the feeling Tzu

Chi members hoped they would inspire in the inhabitants, these houses have become known as "Great Love houses."

Effects and Reflections

Many inhabitants of these villages have remarked, "The moment you walk into a Great Love house, you can feel the loving warmth of a home." In Taiwan, paintings created by members of the Tzu Chi Association of Calligraphers and Painters adorned the walls of every prefabricated house. The paintings were inscribed with a saying of the Master's: "A magnanimous heart is worth more than a spacious house."

With a floor space of forty square meters, though, Great Love houses are not cramped. The quality of these houses is as good, if not better, than that of prefabricated houses built in advanced countries. They set a new standard for the construction of pre-fabricated houses in Taiwan, which was later adopted by the government and other private organizations.

A visit to a Great Love village presents a picture of hope. After night falls, lights glow through the windows of the Great Love houses. Children sit at desks doing their homework; parents pre-pare meals, launder clothes, and hang the washing out to dry; families gather in the living room to watch television and chat. Lights of hope emanate from them all.

42 } *Starting a Tzu Chi chapter from scratch*

CHALLENGE: How can we best serve
those in need who live around us?

"Let us warm the sad, the lonely hearts of others with
our sincerity and eagerness to help." MASTER CHENG YEN

Background

In 1992, my wife and I founded the Vancouver chapter of Tzu Chi
Foundation. As of summer 2008, the organization has donated a
total of over Cdn$24 million, and the number of people we have
served is nearly 800,000. We have over three thousand volunteers serving in the Greater Vancouver area every month.

Master Cheng Yen says: "When you live in a foreign country,
serve the people of that country." How did we, as a pair of new
immigrants, launch a charitable organization with the principles
laid down by the Master?

After Tzu Chi Vancouver was established and we had the first
one hundred volunteers and had collected a good amount of donations—all of which took us less than half a year—we began to
ask: "What is the best way to spend this money?" We had to find
out who needed money most and for what purposes.

The Master also says, "Whatever is taken locally must be used
locally."

We spent a great amount of time on investigation and research prior to kicking off a program. With little knowledge and no network in this new country, we began by looking around ourselves for those that could use our help.

Challenge

We started with the food bank in Vancouver's infamous Downtown Eastside, widely recognized as one of the poorest neighborhoods in Canada. On our first visit, we were surprised to see so many young people in the lineup outside the food bank. Some of these individuals even wore decent clothing.

As new immigrants, we had a lot of questions, such as, "Why don't they get a job?" and, "Why don't they want to work to support themselves?"

We sought to find the answers by talking directly to these people with help from local social workers. We learned that it wasn't that they didn't want to work; they were simply unable to get it. And there wasn't much left of the government's unemployment insurance payout once rent was covered and debts were paid. These people had no choice. They needed help.

As the majority of rations distributed by the food bank were dried goods or packaged foods, fresh fruits and vegetables were what were needed most. We agreed to donate Cdn$1,000 a week for these items. In return, the food bank agreed to let us maintain a station within their Downtown Eastside location.

When we served, we did so with gratitude: "Thank you for letting me serve you!" We used both hands to give out the food. We bowed to those we served and said: "Good morning!" or "Bless you!" or "Have a good day!" We smiled to them, expressing our good wishes and gratitude. Some of our volunteers would stand in line to distribute the food, while others would help single mothers and elderly women carry their bags. Some of those we served had children with them. We would hold the little ones' hands or help them carry things.

Our way of distributing food seemed to be unfamiliar to these people. We were not only serving, but also paying attention to small details. We tried to find ways to make our clients happy. As a result, we were able to build a trustful relationship with our clients in a short period of time.

There are many nice little stories about interactions with our clients. For instance, a gentleman once came and asked us: "Are you Buddhist?"

"Yes, we are Buddhists," I said.

"I am a Catholic," he said. Then he unbuttoned his shirt and took out a cross that he was wearing around his neck. He said: "My God will bless you!"

I also remember a little boy who came to the food bank with his father. While his dad was standing in line, the curious little boy walked around checking out what was being distributed. When he saw there were apples, he yelled in excitement: "Daddy, daddy! Apple, apple!"

Several of our volunteers were so touched that tears came to their eyes. We gave the boy an apple. He took it, looked at us with his bright eyes, and then took a bite of the prized piece of fruit.

Our own children don't eat apples—even if we peel and cut them. Watching this little boy, we realized how blessed we are and how important it is to cherish all that we have. We have come to understand the Master's teaching that when you serve others, you are taught by them.

We started with one food bank station and now we have two stations in Vancouver, two in Burnaby, and one in Surrey. Every week, a team of about twenty volunteers serves in each of these stations.

ANOTHER PROJECT OF the Tzu Chi Vancouver chapter is to assist the Salvation Army every month serving meals to the less fortunate in the Downtown Eastside. We cook the vegetarian meals with great care. On special occasions, we lay tablecloths, light candles, and decorate the settings with flowers, emulating what you might see in a nice restaurant. As usual, we smile and serve the food with both hands while saying blessings to the clients. There is love in every meal we serve. When our guests finish their food, our volunteers in uniform ask, "Coffee or tea?" We hope to make these unfortunate people feel like VIPs once a month. As much as seven to eight hundred people come to each of our lunches.

Initially, we were nervous going to the Downtown Eastside. We were constantly worried that our cars might be broken into, with windows smashed and items stolen. But since we started serving with the Salvation Army, volunteers in Tzu Chi uniform are saluted when they walk down the streets. Our cars are never touched by anyone. We know we've won their trust and friendship. They would even say "Amitabha" (a Buddhist blessing) and use our sign language to say, "Thank you."

During the Chinese New Year, we also distribute "red pockets," the small red envelopes of "lucky money" distributed during the Chinese New Year, and gifts such as shampoo and toothpaste to the people of the Downtown Eastside. Our mission is to ensure that those we serve get exactly the same things we use.

187

We see these people as equals. That's why we buy name brand shampoos or jackets of good quality that we would use ourselves.

The spirit of giving between Tzu Chi volunteers and the recipients does not flow in only one direction. When we were fundraising for victims of an earthquake in Taiwan, many homeless people came to help us. One man searched his bag inside out, hoping to find something he could donate. He found five packs of instant noodles that he had just received from the food bank. He offered to donate all of them. "That's all I have," he said with a smile.

Another homeless friend said he did not have any money and showed us his empty pockets. But he offered to help by calling out to passersby to come and donate. Still another homeless friend said: "I don't have anything, but can I give you a hug so that you can pass it on to the Taiwanese people?"

Effects and Reflections

The Master said people who live a hard life tell us that we must cherish our good fortune. Through serving the people in need, we learn to be grateful.

A homeless woman once started crying after we gave her a bottle of shampoo. "I can finally wash my hair now," she said.

We were all touched by her words. Suddenly, we realized that being able to wash your hair every day is something that could make one cry with joy. We must cherish the simple things we do have. The people we serve are our teachers.

The Master told us that we should wash the feet of the elderly as if we were bathing the Buddha. Those we serve are all buddhas. When we wash their hair, we are bathing the Buddha. When we bring them items they need, we are bringing hopes. When we see smiles on the faces of the less fortunate people we serve, we, too, can't hold back our smiles. It's through this circle of giving with gratitude and respect that we become better people, trusted and loved.

43 } *Project Hope, a model for student-centered schools*

CHALLENGE: How can education transform our world?

"The purpose of Project Hope is to infuse the quake-ravaged regions, the families, children, and the whole of society with hope." MASTER CHENG YEN

Background

Natural disasters not only demolish houses but also cause great damage to schools. In Taiwan, the number of schools affected by the earthquake of 1999 totaled 896, causing a great deal of inconvenience for many schoolchildren. As the Master said, "The hope of a country lies in talent, and the hope of talent lies in education. The hope of parents lies in their children, and the hope of children lies in education." If the reconstruction of the disaster-ravaged schools could not be completed as soon as possible, the students would be unable to receive a regular education and many families would be affected. The Master decided that Tzu Chi would share the burden of school reconstruction in the disaster areas. The Ministry of Education provided a list of more than four hundred quake-damaged schools to choose from, and Tzu Chi committed to rebuild fifty of them.

"Project Hope," as the reconstruction effort was called, aimed not only to rebuild school buildings but also to rekindle hope in children's hearts.

Challenge

Before implementing Project Hope, Tzu Chi was faced with a problem: How could the foundation find enough good architects to plan the building of so many schools? And how could these schools best help students realize their dreams?

On October 8, 1999, after assessing the conditions of the damaged schools in the disaster areas and confirming the number of schools completely destroyed in the earthquake, Tzu Chi invited more than twenty outstanding architects selected from *Taiwan Architect* magazine and Taiwan's National Association of Architects to participate in Project Hope. To be able to take part in such a gigantic project was a dream for all the participants. Tzu Chi emphasized efficiency, but it also communicated closely with all those who were concerned with the project. In the planning stages, the foundation asked representatives from all the schools and parent committees plus architects, technicians, and tradespeople to meetings to discuss details as well as to exchange their ideas and expectations. By way of such discussions, Tzu Chi hoped that a bond would be formed among all the parties and a consensus on the final design would be reached.

In early March 2000, the blueprints for the schools to be reconstructed were finished. The designs Tzu Chi had come up with met requirements for safety, comfort, beauty, and environmental protection, and they also intended to make learning more fun for the students.

Since safety was the top priority, the builders used steel-reinforced concrete to construct only quake-proof schools. Although costly and time-consuming to put up, these structures guarantee safety and durability. Traffic routes in and out of the schools were also reviewed for safety: plans tried to not allow vehicles to drive onto or park on school grounds, and the surrounding roads were closely scrutinized.

To reduce disruptive noise and make the sound environment more comfortable for students and neighborhood residents, the architects placed playgrounds near the street, where most noise is produced, and situated classrooms adjacent to quiet residential districts. In one traffic-filled area, the architect built embankments around the school with the soil left over from the reconstruction of the campus. Other architects also avoided building four-sided enclosed classrooms or corridors that might result in echoes.

All the schools rebuilt by Tzu Chi were designed facing south to maximize sunlight and facilitate ventilation inside the classrooms. Windows were positioned high and low in walls to aid the circulation of air. In order to make the best use of limited space, multifunctional open-air theaters and squares were also built. Furthermore, the classrooms were laid out to facilitate interaction and learning. For example, desks and chairs can be arranged to suit different purposes: in class, students sit facing the blackboard; when they are watching performances, they sit facing the performance area. Other features include larger-than-usual hallways and staircases to ensure maximum safety and ventilation, numerous washrooms, and views and structures sized specifically with a child's height and viewpoint in mind.

Finally, the architects never for a moment forgot that children wanted to hear birds singing and see butterflies dancing in their schools. To make this a reality, they planted more grass and paved the ground with bricks instead of cement to enable the earth to absorb moisture and breathe.

The architects had to solve a lot of problems during the design process. For example, some of the schools were only partly damaged. According to government regulations, school buildings could not be torn down before a certain period of time, so there was some question about how to merge new buildings with old. The Master insisted that all schools be rebuilt keeping their original design and local culture in mind, so they would harmonize with the surroundings. Therefore, the schools rebuilt under Project Hope share one common feature: they all have raised foundations, gables, and slanting roofs, which are major characteristics of traditional buildings in Fujian Province and Taiwan. Combining tradition and modernity, past and present (including stricter building codes), such architectural designs have been created in the hope that they will stand the test of time.

All the Project Hope schools have passed the quality inspection of Tzu Chi's construction department and construction commissioners as well as of contractors and architects. Every Tzu Chi construction commissioner is an expert, and the Master is a perfectionist with previous experience supervising construction projects, which ensures that no work is shoddily done or any inferior building material is used.

Effects and Reflections
By providing students with beautiful learning environments, Project Hope ultimately aimed to help them become upright, intelligent, moral people who harmonize reason, wisdom, and insight and honor goodness, beauty, and truth. It takes unsurpassed professional skill, as well as profound wisdom, to bring this ideal into

being. The architects did their best to blend the school buildings into their natural environments and incorporate human nature in planning every detail so that students could interact more closely with each other and explore and understand nature more fully.

One architect said, "If, when designing a building, we provide for basic human needs, then a positive, interactive atmosphere will certainly be generated between the inhabitants of this space and the environment." A building is more than just a lifeless structural body consisting of steel bars, concrete, pipes, and wires. It can be a space full of life. That's why a building can be called a piece of "solidified music." The purpose of Project Hope was not merely to build schools. It also aimed to create a happy learning environment—like a symphony of vitality, sunshine, and love—for our students. In these schools, no Buddhist influence is visible. All we can see are the Tzu Chi spirit of Great Love, our respect for children, and an authentic manifestation of the unique character and culture of each school.

Developed with Great Love and professional knowledge, Project Hope was intended to shape new hope for education in the quake-ravaged areas and to pave the way for a beautiful future, which is exactly why it attracted so many professionals and experts from different fields.

"Our lives last no more than a few decades," said the Master, "but the schools we rebuild with care will last a lot longer than that. They will cultivate talents for centuries to come."

GARY HO is a property developer and the CEO of the Canadian chapter of the Tzu Chi Foundation, which he founded in 1992. He divides his time between Vancouver, British Columbia, and Taipei.

TZU CHI FOUNDATION CANADA now has seven branches, over 13,000 sponsors, and 1,000 regular volunteers. The Canadian chapter raises more than $1 million every year for charitable causes, including local hospitals, the homeless, and various school boards.

Visit the Buddhist Compassion Relief Tzu Chi Foundation at www.tzuchi.org.